GALAXIES

THE HARVARD BOOKS ON ASTRONOMY

Edited by HARLOW SHAPLEY *and* CECILIA PAYNE-GAPOSCHKIN

ATOMS, STARS, AND NEBULAE
Leo Goldberg and Lawrence H. Aller

OUR SUN
Donald H. Menzel

THE STORY OF VARIABLE STARS
Leon Campbell and Luigi Jacchia

BETWEEN THE PLANETS
Fletcher G. Watson

EARTH, MOON, AND PLANETS
Fred L. Whipple

THE MILKY WAY
Bart J. Bok and Priscilla F. Bok

STARS IN THE MAKING
Cecilia Payne-Gaposchkin

TOOLS OF THE ASTRONOMER
G. R. Miczaika and William M. Sinton

The two Clouds of Magellan and the naked-eye star Achernar. These nearest of external galaxies can be used to locate the south pole of the heavens (cross at bottom of photograph), much as the Pointers of the Big Dipper locate Polaris and the north pole.

Harlow Shapley

GALAXIES

REVISED EDITION

HARVARD UNIVERSITY PRESS

Cambridge, Massachusetts

1961

This book was photocomposed by Graphic Services, Inc., York, Pennsylvania; printed by the Murray Printing Company, Westford, Massachusetts; and bound by the Stanhope Bindery, Boston, Massachusetts.

It was designed by Burton L. Stratton, Marcia Lambrecht Tate, and David Ford, members of the Harvard University Press Production staff.

Preface to the Revised Edition

Since the writing of the first edition of this volume, which was based on the Harris Lectures at Northwestern University, there have been notable advances in the study of galaxies. Large new telescopes have gone into operation, in the Northern Hemisphere on Mount Hamilton and Mount Palomar, and in the south at Pretoria, Canberra, Cordoba, and the Boyden Observatory; the recording and analysis of galaxies is on the programs of all these instruments. The field is currently a very active one because it ties up locally with the Milky Way structural problems and distantly with the basic problems of cosmogony.

It would be possible to double the size of this volume by including a fuller report on investigations in current progress, and by going deeper into the technical details. I have treated only briefly, or not at all, such matters as the beginning of contributions from the radio telescopes, the nature and motions of the arms of spiral galaxies, the important extension to fainter stars of my early color-luminosity arrays for globular clusters, the evidence for the flattening and rotation of irregular galaxies such as that presented by Frank Kerr and G. de Vaucouleurs for the Magellanic Clouds, the details of the red-shift phenomenon, and the new views on the ages and evolution of galaxies and stars, derived from the new-era spectroscopic analyses of stellar atmospheres. These fields are being so busily developed at present that a statement of today may be out-dated tomorrow. Most of what is here reported, however, will better stand the erosion of time.

In the presentation of new material I have been greatly assisted by discussions with many astronomers, and especially with Dr. Walter Baade. Of outstanding usefulness, in reporting the recently acquired knowledge of the composition, motions, and organization of galaxies, have been the epochal treatment of radial velocities and absolute magnitudes by Milton Humason, N. U. Mayall, and A. R. Sandage, and the contributions of A. D. Thackeray and associates at Pretoria (Magellanic Clouds), Erik Holmberg of Sweden (photometry of galaxies), and especially the work on numerous metagalactic problems by F. Zwicky at Palomar.

I am greatly indebted to Mrs. Jacqueline S. Kloss for the preparation of the illustrations for this revised edition, and to Mr. Joseph D. Elder of the Harvard University Press for detailed editorial supervision. My census of the nearer galaxies has been aided over the years by many assistants at the Harvard Observatory in Cambridge and at the George R. Agassiz Station on Oak Ridge. The photographs of the southern sky were made by several observers at the Boyden Station working under the supervision of Dr. J. S. Paraskevopoulos. The continued mapping of the more distant galaxies, which are found to be too numerous for detailed cataloguing, is under way at the Lick, Palomar, and Boyden observatories.

In the work on the strategically located Magellanic Clouds, Mrs. Virginia McK. Nail has collaborated with me in researches on structure, populations, and the variable stars. Our investigations reported in some fifty papers are now serving in a sense as a preface to the studies recently begun with powerful instrumentation at half a dozen southern observatories.

The classification of galaxies has recently been elaborated in considerable detail from the simple systems devised at Lund, Mount Wilson, and Harvard, by W. W. Morgan at the Yerkes Observatory, N. U. Mayall at the Lick Observatory, and G. de Vaucouleurs while at Harvard. Here we shall use only the earlier Hubble system.

Throughout this volume the estimates of distances and luminosities of galaxies have been substantially increased over the values presented in the first edition. Along with these changes have come new estimates of the rate of expansion in the Metagalaxy and of the elapsed time since the expansion began. These important revisions have stemmed from the recognition that our best distance indicators—the cepheid variables—are of at least two kinds: one suitable for the measures of the distances of globular clusters and cluster-type variables, and the other suitable for estimating the distances of the external galaxies and some of the classical cepheids in our own Galaxy.

The contents and structure of our Galaxy are treated rather briefly in this volume because that subject is fully handled in another volume of this series: *The Milky Way,* by B. J. Bok and P. F. Bok. In another book by the writer—*The Inner Metagalaxy* (Yale University Press, 1957)—the distribution of galaxies, and the search for a metagalactic center or boundary, are treated in more detail than in the present nontechnical account. Also, in my compendium of high lights in astronomical progress since 1900, *Source Book in Astronomy, 1900–1950* (Harvard University Press, 1960) are reproduced important contributions by Baade, Eddington, Einstein, Gold, Hubble, Humason, Lemaître, Mayall, and Oort—all of which bear on the problems treated in this book on galaxies.

The recent entry of radio astronomy and photon counters into the investigations of galaxies gives us a fresh view of our problem, a new look at the galaxies both as individuals and as units in the metagalactic structure. Many old metagalactic puzzles, such as the age of the universe, are being partially resolved through combining the techniques of radio and optical astronomy; but, inevitably, new problems, equally difficult, are emerging. Much work lies ahead for observer and theorist. This volume should be regarded as only an introductory step on one road to cosmic understanding.

H. S.

Contents

1   Galactic Explorations   1

Introductory · Interruption for Definitions · The Measurement of Distances to the Stars · The Kinds of Galaxies

2   The Star Clouds of Magellan   27

The Harvard-Peruvian Explorations · The Loop Nebula, Star Clusters, and Peculiar Giant Stars · The Supergiant S Doradus · Distances and Dimensions · On the Future of the Clouds

3   The Astronomical Toolhouse   45

The Abundance of Cepheid Variables · The Period-Luminosity Relation · How Many of the Giant Stars are Cepheids? · What Period is Most Frequent? · An Indicator of Gravitational Potential, or Something · The Light Curves of Cepheids · The Luminosity Curve for Supergiants · Tools That Are Not Sharp Enough

4 The Milky Way As a Galaxy   73

Globular Clusters · From the Heliocentric to the
Galactocentric Hypothesis · The Thickness of the
Galactic System · Measuring the Boundaries ·
More About the Nucleus

5 The Neighboring Galaxies   99

The Triple in Andromeda, and Messier 33 · Distances and Dimensions · Stellar Types in Messier 31
and Messier 33 · Fifty Million Andromedan Novae
on the Way · Two Other Irregular Neighbors ·
Unusual Neighbors in Sculptor and Fornax

6 The Metagalaxy   125

Census of the Inner Metagalaxy · The Region of
Avoidance · The Virgo Cluster of Galaxies · The
Fornax Group of Galaxies, and Others · Faint-
Galaxy Surveys at Harvard, Mount Wilson, Palomar,
and Lick Observatories

7 The Expanding Universe   151

The Space-Density Parameter · Density Gradients ·
The Motions of Galaxies · Red Shifts and Cosmogonies · Trends

   Index   181

Galaxies

1

Galactic Explorations

We who write and read these chapters are setting forth as explorers who rarely touch solid ground or come abreast of contemporary events. Scarcely anything as near as a naked-eye star or as recent as the discovery of America is to be considered. Most of the galactic radiation that comes to our eyes and photographic plates was generated thousands of years before man became curious about his universe. Nevertheless, ours is a practical exploration; the discoveries and deductions are of immediate concern to those who seek orientation in a complicated world. The stars and galaxies are linked with the sun, the sun with light, and light with our living and thinking on the earth's surface. Many times while on excursions

into interstellar space we shall look back, objectively, at the planet where our telescopes are installed. But chiefly we shall be looking far outward into space, and remotely backward and forward in time.

In our swift excursions among the star clouds and galactic systems, we must pause frequently for detailed investigations. The tools of measurement and comprehension must be sharpened, and the new vistas studied in some detail to see where next our explorations can most profitably turn—to see, in fact, if we are getting anywhere. Investigations along the way should not be tedious. The side trips have an interest of their own; and there is a satisfaction in designing instruments for measuring stars and nebulae, as well as using them for measurement and interpretation.

Before we begin the exploration of the sidereal universe and the reporting of what is known about its more distant parts—an excursion that will lead from the Milky Way to the boundaries of measured space—it will be well to define galaxies, describe them preliminarily, and give an account of the way one measures such remote objects. We shall discuss single stars like our sun, describe and use groups of stars like the Pleiades and the rich globular cluster in Hercules, but devote most of our time and space to those yet greater star organizations—the other galaxies that lie beyond the bounds of the Milky Way.

Introductory

In the past as well as recently the great Andromeda spiral has played an important part in solving cosmic mysteries. It is the most conspicuous external galaxy except the Magellanic Clouds, and they are invisible to northern observers. It has been known from ancient times, and appears on the star charts of the Middle Ages. Its diffuseness, and the haziness of some of the brighter globular clusters, inspired Immanuel Kant two centuries ago to a speculation that is now justified. He suggested that at least some of these misty objects, scattered among the clean pointlike stars, might be other distant organizations, themselves composed of myriads of suns; they might well be considered "island universes" in the oceans of empty space, far beyond the confines of the Milky Way system in which our sun and all the naked-eye stars are embedded.

This island-universe hypothesis dimly persisted throughout the nineteenth century, notwithstanding skepticism on the part of a few important astronomers. Sir William Herschel, the founder, near the end of the eighteenth century, of the serious study of galaxies and star clusters, was hesitant. Others shared his doubts. Moreover, it was not an impelling theory; and although a great number of nebulous objects became known through the industrious telescopes of the Hershels, and after the year 1850 numerous spiral forms were discovered among these nebulae, little serious attention was given to the cosmic situation of the various nebulous types. Nobody worried much about them. Theories of the total universe remained dim and unprogressive.

A few astronomical writers of the nineteenth century (Nichol, Proctor, and von Humboldt, for example), playing imaginatively with the island-universe interpretation, introduced and used frequently the term "external galaxy" for those nebulous-appearing sidereal systems that seemed to lie outside our own flat Milky Way star-rich system. It was argued that if some of the faint nebulous objects are really stellar systems, hazy and unresolved because of distance, and if they are comparable in structure with our galactic system, they also could be and should be termed galactic systems, or galaxies. They should be differentiated from the diffuse nebulae, which are of gaseous nature and mostly lie among the stars of our own Galaxy. The Ring Nebula in Lyra (Fig. 1), the Orion Nebula (Fig. 2), the Crab—these are inherently nebulous. They are the true nebulae, and are clearly distinguishable, by location and composition, from the external galaxies. (The terms "extragalactic nebula" and "anagalactic nebula," used by E. P. Hubble and K. Lundmark, respectively, are synonymous with "external galaxy" or simply "galaxy" as used here.) Indeed many galaxies contain various sorts of these true nebulae as minor constituents, along with their stars and star clusters, dust clouds, and clouds of stars.

The cosmic stature and the location in space of galaxies was still uncertain in 1920. Even when their light was analyzed with that most revealing detector, the astronomical spectroscope, and the resulting spectra were found to be like that of the sun—an indication that they probably consist of stars and are not composed of diffuse gases, like the Orion Nebula—even then the astronomers of the nineteenth and early twentieth centuries remained uninterested, and unsure whether the spirals were inside or outside the galactic system. It was hard enough to locate in space the naked-eye stars and measure the nearest parts of the Milky Way. "Near things first"

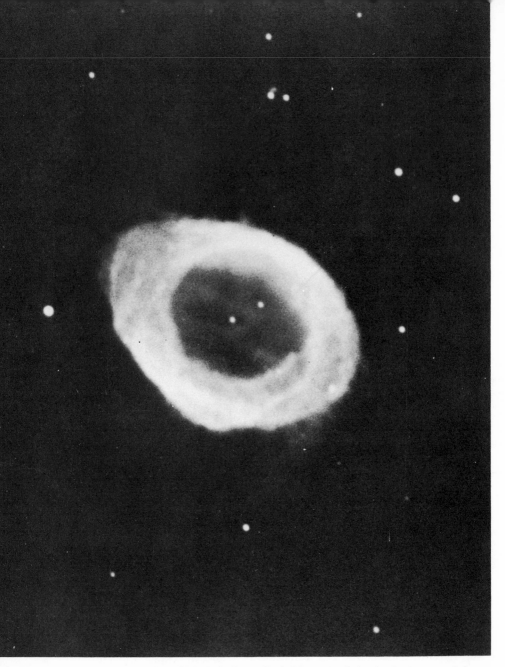

Fig. 1. The Ring Nebula in Lyra. Probably an explosive beginning, certainly an unknown destiny. (Palomar photograph, 200-inch telescope.)

Fig. 2. The Orion Nebula photographed in red light, which gives a picture much like the drawings of a hundred years ago and quite unlike the blue-emulsion photographs now usually published. (Harvard photograph, Rockefeller telescope.)

was the tacit and proper policy. Serious speculation on the horizons of the universe should wait.

Early in this century, however, came more precise and effective work in the measurement of stellar distances. The triangulation methods were much improved; then appeared the photometric methods that will presently be described. First, the photometry of eclipsing double stars began to extend our reach beyond the limits attained by triangulation; then came the estimation of stellar candlepowers, and stellar distances, by employing special characteristics in the spectra of stars; and soon thereafter was developed the powerful method based on cepheid variable stars to which we shall devote much of Chapter 3. With the advent of the measuring tool known as the period-luminosity relation for cepheid variables, the restriction of star-distance measurement to a few hundred light-years, that is, to a few million billion miles, vanished and we were ready to explore the Galaxy and the wide-open extragalactic spaces.

After various photometric criteria of distance had been developed, basically dependent on the cepheid variables, the globular star clusters were explored and their distances found to be astonishingly great. The concept of the galactic system as a stellar discoid with a greatest diameter of only a few thousand light-years was soon abandoned. Our Galaxy, or rather our idea of its size, grew suddenly and prodigiously. The clusters were shown to be affiliated with the galactic system, the center of which was found to lie some tens of thousands of light-years distant in the direction covered by the constellation Sagittarius. The heliocentric hypothesis of the stellar universe had to be abandoned, and the stage was set for further considerations of the nature and location of spiral galaxies.

Meanwhile the speeds of galaxies had been measured spectroscopically (Chapter 7), and the remarkable characteristic known as the *systematic* "red shift" was discovered (page 168). Its interpretation as an indicator of the general recession of the galaxies was widely but not unanimously accepted. For a time the evidence of a measurable angular rotation of the brighter spirals, shown by motions perpendicular to the line of sight and discernible by intercomparison of photographs separated by a short term of years, argued strongly against the acceptance of the great distances indicated by the interpretation of spirals as island universes quite outside our Milky Way system. At great extragalactic distances, any measurable cross motion would have corresponded to unreasonably and disruptively high actual speeds. But the measurements of angular rotation, or of cross motion of any kind, had been difficult and uncertain, and their evidence was discounted when individual cepheid variables were found by E. P. Hubble and others in the nearer spirals. These cepheids immediately made it possible, as we shall show later, to determine the stellar luminosities; and thereby the great distances were confirmed. Spiral nebulae, as H. D. Curtis and Knut Lundmark had ably argued, and as long before them Emanuel Swedenborg, Immanuel Kant, John Michell, and others had suggested, were finally proved to be galaxies, each with its millions of stars.

As soon as cepheid variables and other giant stars in the spirals had been identified, the same methods of distance measurement that some years earlier had been successfully used on the globular clusters were applied in detail by Hubble to the galaxies. The exploring of the space that lies beyond the boundaries of the Milky Way was actively begun. The periods and magnitudes of the cepheid variables, the apparent magnitudes of the brightest invariable stars, the total magnitudes of the galaxies, and their angular diameters— all now became criteria of the distances of galaxies, as previously for globular clusters. No new techniques were necessary; but large telescopes were required, and fast photographic plates, and more careful consideration of the standardization of methods through the more precise study of the motions and luminosities of nearby stars. An important revision of the first standardization is described in Chapter 3, and throughout this edition appropriate corrections to earlier values are applied. Later it transpired that the red shift (recession speed) is a rough indicator of distance.

So much for a rapid survey of a rapidly developing subject. A proper introduction to the galaxies should also contain a few further paragraphs on the techniques of measuring stellar distances and galactic dimensions. But first a digression to clarify the terminology. Fortunately, most of the language of the astronomy of galaxies is common talk. The explanation of technical words and phrases can therefore be brief.

Interruption for Definitions

Magnitude is the astronomical term for indicating brightness, not size. Actually, stellar magnitude is the logarithm (on a special base) of the faintness. The larger the magnitude numerically, the fainter the star. For example, a few of the brightest naked-eye stars are of the first magnitude; the faintest seen with the unaided eye are of the sixth magnitude; the faintest visible with the largest telescopes are near the eighteenth magnitude, and the faintest stars that such telescopes can now photograph, about the twenty-fourth magnitude. The difference between the *apparent magnitude* of a star (how bright it looks to us) and the *absolute magnitude* (how bright it really is at unit distance) becomes important in the measurement of distance, as is shown later in this chapter.

With a *spectroscope,* containing a prism or comparable light-dispersing device, the radiation from a star or galaxy can be spread into the various colors of which the light is composed, each color with its characteristic wavelength. (For an account of spectroscopes and other starlight-analyzing equipment, see another volume in this series, *Tools of the Astronomer,* by G. R. Miczaika and W. M. Sinton.) This streak or band of colored light—the spectrum—is generally crossed by dark lines produced by specialized light absorption in the stellar atmospheres above the principal radiating surface of the star. The pattern of absorption lines varies from star to star, and we therefore have many *spectral classes,* indicative of the various temperatures, sizes, densities, and atmospheric conditions. The most common spectral classes carry the designations *B, A, F, G, K, M*—a series arranged in the order of decreasing surface temperature. Subdivisions are indicated numerically, 0 to 9; thus: *A*5, *G*0, *K*9.

The difference between a blue photographic magnitude and a yellow photographic magnitude is the *color index.* Color indices and spectral classes are closely correlated. For example, large color indices indicate red stars of spectral classes *K* and *M;* the intermediate color indices, like that of the sun, are associated with stars of classes *F* and *G;* and the small color indices refer to bluish stars of classes *B* and *A.*

The lines in the spectra of many stars and galaxies are shifted away from their normal positions. Interpreted on the basis of the Doppler principle, this shift shows motion of the radiating object along the line of sight. The motion is away from the observer (*positive radial velocity*) if the spectral lines show a *red shift*—a shift, that is, toward the red end of the spectrum, toward the longer-wavelength side of the normal position of the lines; the object is approaching if the shift is toward the blue end of the spectrum (negative radial velocity).

Radial motions, along the line of sight, are commonly expressed in miles or kilometers per second. The cross motion, at right angles to the line-of-sight, called the *proper motion,* is measured in angular units —degrees, minutes, and seconds of arc—per year or per century.

Stellar distances are measured by *trigonometric* and *photometric* methods. The *parallax* of a star is the angle subtended at the star by the radius of the earth's orbit (about 93 million miles). The smaller the parallax, the greater the distance (Fig. 3). Represented in

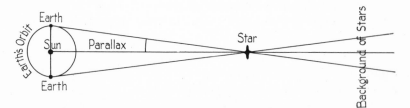

Fig. 3. A diagram that may help to define "parallax," the distance-indicating angle, and suggest the standard method of locating the nearer stars.

Fig. 4. The long-focus parallax-measuring refractor of the Van Vleck Observatory of Wesleyan University.

seconds of arc, the parallax is numerically the reciprocal of the distance expressed in the unit called a *parsec*. Thus a *parallax* of 1 *sec*ond of arc (1″) corresponds to a distance of 1 parsec. A parallax of 0″.1 means a distance of 10 parsecs; 0″.001, 1000 parsecs, and so on. A telescope devoted to parallax measurement is shown in Fig. 4.

Photometrically measured distances are those that are based on measures of the quantity of light. There are many kinds of *photometers,* some directly employing the human eye (visual), others used with the astronomical camera (photographic), and, most sensitive of all, those using phototubes (photoelectric) and photon counters. Ordinarily the photographic records of star brightness are made in blue light, but yellow-sensitive and red-sensitive photographic plates provide "yellow" and "red" magnitudes, and their use is increasing as the speeds of photographic emulsions are increased.

The distance light travels in a year, the *light-year,* is the distance unit most commonly used in this volume; it is equivalent to 5.88 trillion miles. One parsec equals 3.26 light-years, or a little over 19 trillion miles. The *kiloparsec* and the *megaparsec,* which are the convenient units for measuring the distances of galaxies, are a thousand and a million parsecs, respectively.

Right ascension and *declination* are the astronomer's usual coordinates for locating positions in the sky. They are analagous to longitude and latitude on the surface of the earth. Declinations north of the equator are positive; south, negative.

The *galactic longitude* and *galactic latitude* constitute an alternative system, which is used to indicate position in the sky with respect to the Milky Way. The equator of this system is the galactic circle; its north pole is in the constellation Coma Berenices, and its south pole is in Sculptor.

In the *numbering* and *naming* of star clusters, nebulae, and galaxies, the letters NGC and IC refer to the *New General Catalogue* of J. L. E. Dreyer and its indices, respectively (page 126). A hundred of the brighter objects were previously catalogued by Charles Messier (page 74), and bear his name (frequently abbreviated to M), as well as the NGC number. Thus the Andromeda Nebula is M 31 = NGC 224.

Cepheid variable stars, named for their prototype Delta Cephei, are now generally recognized as single high-luminosity stars that periodically swell up and shrink, with consequent periodic variations in light, color, temperature, spectral class, and other characteristics. The pulsations make cepheids easy to discover because their magnitudes are continuously changing. They are giant and supergiant stars and therefore stand out conspicuously among the brighter stars of a globular cluster or a galaxy. When the period of a cepheid is less than a day, the variable is commonly called a

Fig. 5.   The southern globular cluster No. 55 in Messier's catalogue. (Harvard photograph, Rockefeller telescope.)

cluster variable, because stars of this sort were first found abundantly in globular star clusters (Fig. 5); a synonym is RR Lyrae variable. The other two principal types of variable stars are the *eclipsing binaries* and the *long-period variables,* neither of which plays an important role in the discussion of galaxies.

The *novae* are relatively short-lived phenomena, but violent. They are stars that usually begin their variations explosively (Fig. 59); after a temporary brilliance they fade away gradually, but sometimes convulsively.

The *period* of a variable star is the average interval of time required for the variable to go through one complete cycle of its changes. The period is generally reckoned from maximum to maximum of light for cepheid and long-period variables, and from minimum to minimum for eclipsing binaries.

The *light curve* of a variable is a graph showing the course of the variations in brightness. Usually the stellar magnitude is plotted as vertical coordinate and time, in hours or days or period lengths, as horizontal coordinate. Typical light curves appear in Figs. 22, 32, 33, 57, and 59. A *velocity curve* delineates the variations in velocity as revealed by spectrum-line shifts.

The *Metagalaxy* is the all-inclusive system of galaxies, clusters, nebulae, stars, planets, interstellar gas and dust, and radiation; it is practically identical with the material universe.

The Measurement of Distances to the Stars

Our isolation in the vacuum of surrounding space obviously prevents any use in stellar measurement of the surveyor's rods and chains; but the isolation does not hinder the use of the surveyor's triangulation method, at least for our planets and the nearby stars.

The terrestrial surveyor, when measuring the distance to some inaccessible mark, such as a distant mountain peak, establishes on the earth's surface a long triangle that has the mark at its vertex. He measures the length of the short side of the triangle and with telescopic pointings from the ends of this base line he gets the angles necessary for the solution of his terrestrial triangle and for the calculation of the distance to the selected mark.

For measuring the distance to a nearby star the sidereal surveyor sets up his base line in the solar system (see Fig. 3). He generally uses the diameter of the earth's orbit—a base line of 186 million miles; and his telescopic pointings at appropriate times of the year (usually at about 6-month intervals) give him the directions to the nearby star and provide the celestial triangle which is used to calculate the distance.

In principle, the triangulation for stellar distances is simple. In practice, it is very difficult; and it fails altogether, or is of little weight, when distances exceed 1000 light-years, chiefly because of instrumental limitations and inescapable observational errors. Indeed, to get reliable distances of 100 light-years requires exceedingly high accuracy of measurement. Under the inspiration and leadership of Kapteyn of Holland, and especially of Schlesinger of Yale, precise photographic methods of measuring angles on the sky have been developed, special telescopes have been constructed, and, since 1910, from the observatories in America, Europe, and South Africa have come relatively accurate trigonometric determinations of the distances of a few thousand stars. The work is basic. It is almost indispensable in preparing the tools for the measurement of the remoter parts of the universe; but such triangulation does not directly help us at all when we would survey the roads to star clouds and galaxies, for none of them is within its limited reach.

If the triangulation method alone were available, our task of measuring the distances to galaxies would appear hopeless. Looking at the Milky Way, we see, even with small telescopes, thousands of stars that are beyond our range; but how far beyond we would not know if trigonometry were our sole resource. Even some of the naked-eye stars are too remote for triangulation. *Indirectly,* however, the trigonometric measures of the nearby stars lead us to the Milky Way; they calibrate more potent methods.

It is fortunate that in the solar neighborhood the survey of the near and attainable stars can provide a straightforward standardization of the widely usable photometric method of measuring stellar distances. It might have been otherwise. There are many regions in the Milky Way where such standardization, or even the photometric method itself, would be complicated, precarious, and perhaps impossible. The chaotic dark and bright nebulae, such as that shown in Fig. 6, involve stars and planets that are badly situated as headquarters for reliable measurements of space.

The photometric method, like the trigonometric, is simple in principle but intricate in practice, and sometimes confusing and fallacious. In one sentence we can explain the method by saying that if in some way we know the real brightness of a star (its candlepower, or *absolute magnitude*), we can calculate the distance after we measure the *apparent magnitude,* which is a measure of the quantity of the star's spreading light that reaches us across intervening space. For example, $\log d = 0.2\ (m - M) + 1$, where d is distance in parsecs, and m and M are apparent and absolute magnitudes, respectively. An uncertainly estimated δm must be added to the apparent magnitude to allow for dust-and-gas dimming. A familiar illustration is the estimating of the relative distances of street lights from their relative apparent brightnesses after we know that their candlepowers (actual brightnesses) are all the same. Dimness is an indicator of distance.

But there are difficulties. In the first place, the stars differ greatly in candlepower. Some are 10,000 times brighter than the sun, some 10,000 times fainter (Fig. 7), and not many of them are actually and clearly tagged with their absolute magnitudes (candlepowers). Also, the *apparent* magnitudes of stars are difficult to measure accurately; and the dust and gas of the space between us and the stars sometimes seriously dim the light in transmission, so that the simple formulas that apply to clear space do not hold.

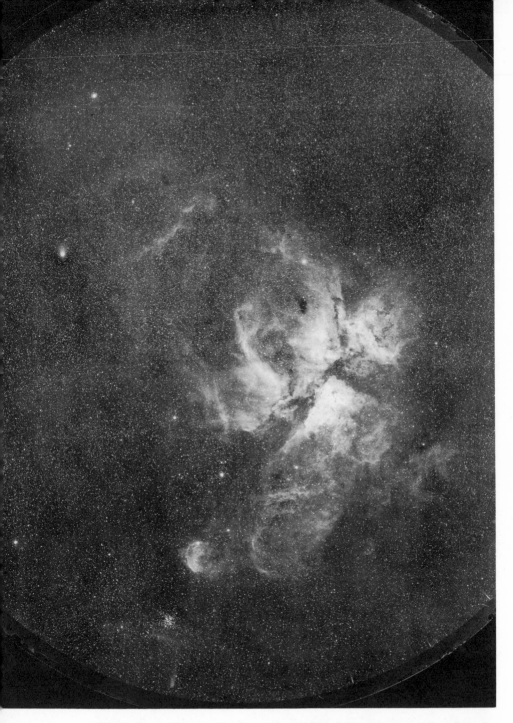

Fig. 6. Interstellar gases in the southern Milky Way, in part the aftereffect of a century-old explosion of the star Eta Carinae. (Harvard photograph, ADH telescope.)

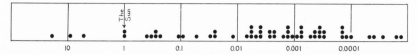

Fig. 7. Van de Kamp's plotting of the frequency of relative luminosities locates the sun with respect to the nearer stars; most of our neighbors are seen to be dwarfs in luminosity.

Notwithstanding such difficulties, the photometric method is practicable and widely used; it can be applied not only to stars, but, as we have already noted, to globular clusters, and even to galaxies of stars. And once we learn to estimate accurately the total candlepower of an average galaxy—the total luminosity of its population of millions of stars—we can dispense with the use of individual stars such as cepheids, and, using instead this average candlepower of a whole galaxy, penetrate space with a new photometric measuring rod to distances a million times greater than those possible when our reliance was placed wholly on trigonometric methods. The principle of photometric measurement of stellar distances is as old as Newton, or older; but its practical development and use are recent and revolutionary. Without it, the existence of external galaxies would have remained hypothetical, and modern cosmogony could not have existed.

The power of the photometric method lies in the developing of ways of estimating accurately the candlepowers of stars of those various types that are easily identifiable and are widely spread throughout the universe. To estimate great distances, we must first find the *absolute* brightnesses of stars that are of such great inherent radiance that they can be seen or photographed at such distances. Procedures relevant to this art will be described in Chapters 3 and 4.

As soon as we find the distances of the nearer galaxies, we can measure their angular dimensions and compute diameters in miles or in light-years. With sizes known, we proceed to intercompare the various galaxies. Finding much variety, we are immediately led to the setting up of types or classes. From that point the procedure is clear, and the questions ask themselves: What is the number of galaxies, how many kinds are there, what is their distribution in space, what are their relations to each other and to our own galaxy? Are they star factories? What of their internal activities, their forms, composition, origin, ages, destiny?

With such questions we are getting too far ahead of our story; moreover, the questions are too many, and at the present time too largely unanswerable. But in this preliminary chapter a description of the kinds of galaxies is appropriate, as is also a comment on their numbers.

The Kinds of Galaxies

Galaxies show much diversity in brightness and in size. There are titanic systems, such as the Andromeda Nebula, which are almost a thousand times as bright and voluminous as dwarf systems like the Sculptor galaxy (Chapter 5). These two neighboring objects represent extremes in brightness, the average galaxy being about halfway between in absolute magnitude and number of stars.

Since there is a large spread in real brightness, there results in any survey of external systems brighter than a given apparent magnitude a preference for the most luminous. The dwarfs are systematically overlooked. We must be cautious, therefore, with such statements as "three-fourths of the galaxies are of the spiral type," because among the dwarf systems, most of which are not easily photographed in detail, the relative abundance of the various types may be otherwise than for galaxies of an average brightness, or for giant systems. Indeed, the *average* galaxy in a survey based on apparent brightness may differ considerably in type, as in luminosity, from the average galaxy in a given volume of space wherein everything is known.

To illustrate this rather important point by an astronomical analogy, we note that, when the stars visible to the unaided eye are listed in order of absolute luminosity, the sun appears to be less luminous than the average star. That position is certainly correct if we are dealing only with naked-eye stars—the sun is relatively dwarfish. But when we compare the sun with *all* stars, naked-eye and telescopic, that are in the neighborhood of the sun, it is found to be far above the average in brightness (Fig. 7). Careful research has revealed great numbers of dwarf stars. Probably the conditions found in our immediate neighborhood hold generally in the outer parts of the Milky Way, and possibly even in the distant central nucleus. Dwarf stars may predominate almost everywhere.

About 75 percent of the *brighter* galaxies so far satisfactorily observed and classified belong to the spiral type. The spirals generally show a bright nucleus, which is more or less spheroidal, and a flatter outer portion in which spiral arms are a conspicuous feature. The whole galaxy is watch-shaped, or more frequently wheel-shaped, with a conspicuous hub.

About 20 percent of the brighter galaxies are of the spheroidal or ellipsoidal type, radially symmetric about the center, or about an axis through the center, with indefinite boundaries, and no arms or other conspicuous structural detail.

The remainder of the brighter galaxies are irregular in structure and in form (the Magellanic type), or are peculiar variants on spiral and spheroidal types.

The percentages 75, 20, and 5 for spirals S, ellipsoidals (or spheroidals) E, and irregulars I, respectively, are proper for a superficial survey of galaxies, such as for the thousand brightest as recorded in the Shapley-Ames catalogue. They are, however, not the correct percentages when a total count is made for a given volume of space, for then the fainter spheroidals and irregulars appear abundantly and the correct percentages may be more like 30, 60, and 10.

The illustrations that appear throughout this volume show that the spiral and spheroidal galaxies can be readily subdivided. Knut Lundmark, of the Lund University Observatory in Sweden, and E. P. Hubble of the Mount Wilson Observatory, among others, have made classifications applicable to the brighter objects, and have introduced symbols and names to describe the various categories. These two systems of classification are similar in principle and detail; but the English astronomer J. H. Reynolds has appropriately emphasized the fact that practically every galaxy is distinguishable from all others; the classifications are only convenient shelves, not to be taken too seriously. (Classifications by Morgan and Mayall and by de Vaucouleurs are mentioned below.) The symbols used in this book for the brighter galaxies are those employed by Hubble, but the names differ in some details; he used "elliptical" for our "spheroidal," and "extragalactic nebula" for our term "galaxy." Although by the writer and many others the term "galaxy" is preferred to "extragalactic nebula," the adjective "nebular" is found useful sometimes in referring to the faint nebulous objects that appear in the surveys of distant external galaxies. Strict and strained consistency of usage is avoided in the following pages.

Detailed descriptions, especially the subclassification of spheroidal and spiral galaxies given below, are possible only for those systems near enough for large-scale photography. For 95 percent of the galaxies shown in the Harvard surveys, such classification is not possible. They are too faint and structureless. For them we have the Bruce-telescope system of classes, based on two parameters: (1) the *degree of central condensation* (six categories from *a* for no concentration to *f* for the highest observed) and (2) the *form of the photographed image* (ten categories from 10 for circular outline to 1 for extreme elongation). Thus *a*9 indicates a smooth nearly circular image; *f*1, an image one-tenth as wide as long and highly concentrated into a starlike nucleus; *e*5*s*, an object of intermediate concentration half as wide as long and showing indications of spiral arms. The Bruce system could be used also, if desired, for the brighter objects by supplementing the letter-number code with *s* for spiral, *i* for irregular, and so on; but the classification by Hubble is easier, and temporarily sufficient.

Spheroidals. The brighter spheroidal galaxies are subclassified at present according to the shape of the projected image. With more detailed knowledge of the concentration of light and the types of stars in a spheroidal galaxy, they can no doubt be further subclassified, or at least ordered in a two-demensional plan, such as proves to be practicable in the Bruce classification of all faint galaxies.

When classifying bright spheroidals, following Hubble's notation, we denote a circular image by $E0$; it may be the image of a truly spherical object, or of an oblate one viewed flat side on (Fig. 8). The oblateness of a spheroidal galaxy is easily accounted for, if we accept a common hypothesis that flattening of a gaseous, liquid, or stellar spheroid is the result and measure of rotation about an axis. Gravity and centrifugal force combine to produce the distortion.

A very elongated spheroidal system ($E7$) is of course an extremely oblate wheel-shaped object seen on edge. (It is not at all likely to be a cigar-shaped object, because of the inherent instability of such a form under gravitational forces.) In the intermediate classes of spheroidal galaxies, $E1$ to $E6$, tilt and oblateness are involved in varying degree. For any given object we can only say that it is at least as flat as it appears, and probably much flatter. Statistical arguments can be used to draw some rather uncertain conclusions about the relative frequency of the different degrees of flattening.

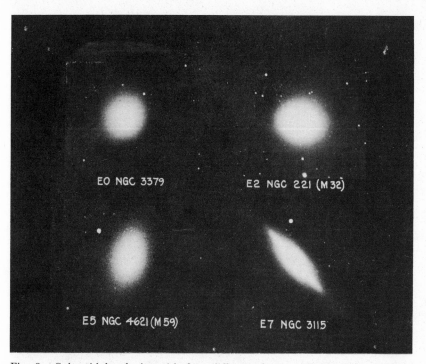

Fig. 8. Spheroidal galaxies with four different degrees of oblateness. (Mount Wilson photographs by Hubble, 100-inch telescope.)

In the future, precise measures of the velocities within a spheroidal galaxy, and a careful study of the degree of concentration of light along the different radii, may help to disentangle tilt from oblateness. At present, surmise does not seem important. The distribution of tilt can be more profitably studied among the spirals, which are unquestionably flat.

For distant galaxies it is difficult to discriminate between the elongated *E*7 spheroidal system and some of the edgewise spirals that show little detail of internal structure and no granulation into stars, clusters, and nebulosity. In fact, when arranged in a sequence there is perhaps intrinsically little difference between these two types, and Hubble has proposed a connectant form, *S*0, representing the faintest discernible stage of spiraling.

Spirals. In classifying bright spirals, we start the series with *Sa*, in which arms can be clearly detected or reasonably surmised. There is little detail shown. The class *Sb* refers to objects with arms more distinct, perhaps more openly spread (Fig. 9). The structural

Fig. 9.   The terrestrial observer is almost exactly in the equatorial plane of this spiral galaxy, which bears the catalogue number NGC 4565. (Mount Wilson photograph, 200-inch telescope.)

Fig. 10. Number 83 in Messier's catalogue, a class *Sc* spiral, is convincing in its spectacular evidence that the universe is not static. (Harvard photograph, Rockefeller telescope.)

detail and clustering, obvious in the arms of class *Sb*, become still more pronounced in the wide-open type, *Sc*, of which the great Messier 83 (Fig. 10), is a luminous example. We can go one stage further and use *Sd* for the most spread-out spirals (such as that shown in Fig. 11), in which the nucleus is conspicuous and the spiral arms are much broken and relatively dim. The symbols *Sab*, *Sbc*, and *Scd* denote intermediate forms. In all these spiral classes the arms emanate from the center of the galaxy, or from very near the center.

A few additional notes will complete this introduction to the galaxies:

1. There is a series of spiral forms, paralleling the normal type just described, in which the arms originate from the edge of a central disk rather than from a concentrated central nucleus. Fre-

Fig. 11. Of the million galaxies recorded at the Harvard Observatory, this one is Number 4, discovered a century ago as a disappointment during a search for comets. The catalogue number is NGC 7793, the class is *Sd*, and the distance is about 5 million light-years. Outlying fragments of the galaxy are scattered over the whole field. (Harvard photograph, Bruce telescope.)

quently the arms start from the ends of a luminous bar that crosses the nucleus and surrounding disk (Fig. 12). These so-called barred spirals are designated *SBa, SBb,* and *SBc,* with *SBab* and *SBbc* for intermediates.

2. The *arms* are not the whole of the outer structure of the spirals; they are in fact merely enhancements on the background of light (stars) surrounding the nucleus, and are populated with young supergiant stars and nebulae. We shall see later that the total light contributed by what is generally recognized as the spiral arms is but a small portion of the total extranuclear light, much as coronal streamers seen at total solar eclipses are now known to be chiefly high lights on the background of the luminous globular coronas.

3. Some external galaxies are without a visible central nucleus. Either no nucleus exists or it is hidden behind heavy obscuring dust. (For an example, see Fig. 88 of chapter 7.)

4. All of the various subclasses, *Sa, SBc, E*5, and the others, include some forms considerably divergent from the average. The classification here used is obviously preliminary and useful chiefly for temporary guidance. Asymmetries exist; many intermediates lie between average forms, and chaotically irregular objects like the Magellanic Clouds are well known, as are also double galaxies (Fig. 13) and groups. An elaborate classification, based chiefly on form and arm structure, has been devised by G. de Vaucouleurs; and an important analytic classification involving spectrum features and star types, as well as structure and degree of concentration, has been developed by W. W. Morgan, who bases his system largely on spectroscopic work by himself and N. U. Mayall and on Hubble's large collection of galaxy photographs.

5. The possibility of arranging the kinds of bright galaxies into one sequence, *E*0–7, *S*0, *Sa–d, I,* is not to be taken as a proof that one type develops into an adjacent form. We have here a "series of convenience," not necessarily an evolutionary tree. It is a little too early in the study of galaxies to yield without reserve to the temptation to evolve one type from another.

It will appear later that hundreds of thousands of galaxies have now been photographed, but that only a few hundred are near enough to be studied in some detail. Perhaps a dozen or fifteen are within 2 million light-years (the census of dwarf galaxies is not complete, even to that small distance). In the vast material before

Fig. 12. NGC 7741 is a barred spiral with a complicated nucleus. (Palomar photograph, 200-inch telescope.)

Fig. 13. Messier 60 and NGC 4647, a pair of unlike galaxies too remote for detailed analysis. (Mount Wilson photograph, 100-inch telescope.)

us we find that the most satisfying of all galaxies for exploration are the Clouds of Magellan. The two following chapters will be devoted to these irregular systems. They are not only the nearest, but also the richest in procurable observational data, and in suggestion.

2

The Star Clouds
of Magellan

The astronomy of galaxies would probably
have been ahead by a generation, perhaps by
50 years, if Chance, or Fate, or whatever it is
that fixes things as they are had put a typical
spiral and a typical spheroidal galaxy in the
positions now occupied by the Large and Small
Magellanic Clouds. If a spiral such as the one
listed as NGC 4647 (Fig. 13) were, like them,
only 160,000 light-years away, and its giant
and supergiant stars were therefore easy to
observe for motions and spectral characteristics, many of the dilemmas of the past 40
years would never have arisen. We should
have known long ago whether spiral arms
wind up, or unwind, or neither; whether they
are superficial in galactic structure, or basic.

And for more than 100 years we should have known that the spirals are star-filled external galaxies, and neither mysterious nebulous constituents of our own Milky Way system, as was once surmised, nor planetary systems in formation.

Similarly, if a spheroidal galaxy like Messier 60 (Fig. 13) were only 160,000 light-years distant, we probably should have been spared many labors and doubts concerning such objects. Long ago we might have known, if we had given proper effort to the inquiry, something of the inner structure, perhaps even the laws of internal motions in spheroidal galaxies. We might have known definitely whether they are free of interstellar dust. We should have better understood their relation to globular clusters on the one hand and to the nuclei of spiral galaxies on the other. But, as it is, such problems are even now largely unsolved, because typical spheroidal galaxies are very remote and therefore difficult to analyze.

The Andromedans have better luck! Those hypothetical investigators located in the great Andromeda Nebula (Messier 31) have two small spheroidal galaxies close at hand, and the fine open spiral Messier 33 only half a million light-years away. They are spared our fortune of having as our nearest neighbors two irregular star clouds that for many years masqueraded before us as fragments detached from the Milky Way. Only gradually have we given these Clouds of Magellan the status of external systems and begun to appreciate that through their study we are analyzing an interesting but not very frequent form of galaxy (Fig. 14). The study of their irregular structures and motions gives little help in solving problems of the nature and operation of spheroidal and spiral galaxies. But we must make the best of what we have, and it will soon appear that the best is indeed good. It's marvelous.

Cape Clouds they were called by the fifteenth-century Portuguese navigators, who picked them up in the southern sky as their ships approached the Cape of Good Hope. These unprecedented "Little Clouds" were, in fact, of some navigational use because they and the south pole of the heavens are at the three vertices of a nearly equilateral triangle; that is, they help locate the south pole. The oddity of them was described by Peter Martyr: "Coompasinge abowte the poynt thereof . . . certeyne shynynge whyte cloudes here and there amonge the starres, like unto theym whiche are seene in

Fig. 14.   The Small Magellanic Cloud, R.A. 0ʰ 50ᵐ, Dec. −73°. To the right of this important and useful galaxy is the giant globular cluster 47 Tucanae. (Harvard photograph, ADH telescope.)

the tracte of heaven cauled Lactea via, that is the mylke whyte waye."

Corsali reports: "Manifestly twoo clowdes of reasonable bygnesse movynge abowt the place of the pole continually now rysynge and now faulynge, so keepynge theyr continuall course in circular movynge, with a starre ever in the myddest which is turned abowt with them abowte .xi. degrees frome the pole."

Variously designated by the navigators, the peculiar objects became indelibly associated in the literature of astronomy with the Great Circumnavigator. Only occasionally does an astronomer resort to the names Nubecula Major and Nubecula Minor. Magellan's associate and historian, Pigafetta, described the Clouds officially, during the course of that first round-the-world tour of 1518–1520, and thus made it appropriate to attach the explorer's name to these nearby galaxies that we ourselves now propose to explore.

The smaller of the two Clouds lies in the constellation of the Toucan. The Large Cloud is chiefly in Dorado, the Goldfish. Both

Clouds spread beyond the boundaries of the constellations in which they chiefly lie. They illuminate a region of the sky romantically touched with exotic birds and beasts, if we judge by the constellation names. The water snake, the phoenix, the flying fish are there with the flamingo, the chameleon, the Indian fly, and the bird of paradise. All are near the south pole of the heavens, where to most of us the constellations are unfamiliar.

It would have been more convenient if the Magellanic Clouds were situated much farther north. Their cosmographic position has delayed their exploration, for there are ten observatories in the Northern Hemisphere to one in the Southern. Up to 1940 the southern stations of two American observatories, Harvard and Lick, had to do practically all the work on these important systems. The convenience of terrestrial astronomers obviously was not consulted in laying out the Metagalaxy.

The Harvard-Peruvian Explorations

When the Clouds of Magellan are observed with the unaided eye, or visually inspected with any of the southern telescopes, or photographed with only moderate power, they appear not very large. The Small Cloud is then recorded as less than 4° in diameter; the Large, less than 8°, and dominated by a densely populated off-center bar or axis. Both are comparable in apparent size with some of the individual star clouds in our Milky Way, such as the bright patches of galactic light in Cygnus, Scutum, and Sagittarius. Such unpenetrating early views showed nevertheless, a considerable amount of irregularity in form and in star density; but they were not especially revealing. Even as late as the beginning of this century the French writer Camille Flammarion summed up knowledge of the Large Cloud by saying that it contained 291 distinct nebulae, 46 clusters, and 582 stars. Descriptions such as this gave little suggestion of the deep significance and the tremendous richness of our nearest external galaxy, for they merely reported the occasional observations by Sir John Herschel and by a few other scientific voyagers to the Southern Hemisphere.

It was not until the growing Harvard Observatory had an opportunity in the eighteen nineties to develop a southern station, and also had the good fortune of a substantial gift from Miss Catherine Bruce of New York, that the Magellanic Clouds began

Fig. 15. The Bruce telescope building (and El Misti) at the Arequipa Station of the Harvard Observatory, 1899–1926.

to unfold their story and inaugurate the astronomy of the galaxies. The Bruce photographic refractor (Figs. 15 and 16) came into existence through the cooperative efforts of Alvan Clark and Professor Pickering and their colleagues; it was in operation in Peru before 1900. This 24-inch large-field refractor, an exceedingly powerful instrument for its day, is now on the shelf. Its revised mounting carries the novel ADH Baker-Schmidt astrograph, one of the most active and effective of southern telescopes for the study of stars, star clouds, and galaxies.

There were many urgent jobs 60 years ago for the new Bruce refractor, which could photograph stars considerably fainter than the sixteenth magnitude in an hour's exposure, and could cover a field, on a single photographic plate, as extensive as the bowl of the Big Dipper. It had the responsibility of covering the whole southern sky—of doing much pioneering work along the rich southern Milky Way. For the Magellanic Clouds, therefore, the program proceeded slowly and it was several years before anything more significant was observed on the photographic plates than large numbers of star clusters and gaseous nebulae, such as were

Fig. 16. The Bruce telescope in Cambridge before its going to the Southern Hemisphere.

expected from the earlier visual observations by Sir John Herschel and others, and not hundreds but tens of thousands of stars.

The Clouds had been looked at for 400 years, but only now at the turn of the century were they beginning to be clearly seen. They were at last being accurately observed, but not by an ardent stargazer on the quarter-deck of an exploring frigate; not by the celestial explorer at his temporary observing station in Australia, South Africa, or South America; not even by the Harvard astronomer laboriously exposing large photographically sensitive plates in a powerful camera at the foot of El Misti in Peru. The Clouds were first being really seen by a young woman sitting at a desk in Cambridge, Massachusetts, holding in her hand an eyepiece with which she could examine a confusion of little black specks on a glass plate.

Miss Henrietta S. Leavitt of the staff of the Harvard Observatory had the gift of seeing things and of making useful records of her measures. She began by finding in the Magellanic Clouds the miracle variable stars that have subsequently turned out to be extremely significant both for the exploration of extragalactic space and for the measurement of star distances throughout our own Milky Way system.

She and other early workers on the Bruce plates had of course no way of knowing that the starlight from the Magellanic Clouds was some 1600 centuries old. In the first decades of the career of the Bruce telescope, distances of 160,000 light-years were quite unbelievable. But it is not uncommon for scientists to make systematic measures without knowing exactly what they measure. If the measures are good, those who make them can feel sure that significant interpretation will one day be forthcoming.

For Solon I. Bailey and Miss Leavitt, the two leaders in the discovery of the distant variable stars that were revealed by the Bruce telescope and the other Harvard Observatory instruments (Fig. 17),

Fig. 17. The ADH telescope in South Africa. The Bruce telescope at the Boyden Station of the Harvard Observatory was replaced in 1952 by the Armagh-Dunsink-Harvard Baker-Schmidt instrument, which is one of the most effective telescopes in the Southern Hemishpere. (Photograph by the *Friend* of Bloemfontein.)

the immediate goal was the detection of variations in the intensity of starlight. Professor Bailey specialized on the star clusters, Miss Leavitt on the Clouds of Magellan. In 1906 she published a list of newly discovered faint variable stars in the two Magellanic Clouds —808 in the Large Cloud and 969 in the Small. The positions of these stars were recorded in appropriate coordinates, and also their maximum and minimum magnitudes, referred to preliminary standards. It was not then noted that the range was generally about one magnitude, whether the variable star was among the brightest objects in the Clouds or among the faintest recorded by the photographic plate. There the matter rested for a bit, and we also shall let it rest until the next chapter, wherein come under discussion the astronomical tools that the astronomers have been able to fashion from the analysis of these nearby irregular galaxies.

Continuing the description of the Magellanic Clouds, we note that in addition to their very numerous variable stars there is within them a good sprinkling of many other stellar types. Their variable stars are duplicated in kind in our galactic system, even among the naked-eye neighbors of the sun. Similarly, the red giants of the solar neighborhood, the blue giants, and other highly luminous stars that have various spectral peculiarities, all find their counterparts in the Clouds. The Axis or Bar of the Large Cloud (Fig. 18) resembles somewhat the inner structure of some of the barred spirals.

Miss Annie J. Cannon's early work on the spectra of the brightest stars in the Clouds revealed among those of the common spectral classes a considerable number of important peculiar stars. In our own galactic system such stars are located chiefly, if not exclusively, in the thick of the Milky Way band—rarely, if ever, in the high latitudes, at large angular distances from the galactic circle. Since the Clouds stand well clear of the Milky Way, we can in consequence separate their peculiar stars from the abundant superposed ordinary stars of our own system. If a star of a peculiar type, such as a nova, a "classical" cepheid, a P Cygni or Class O star, is found in the direction of the Magellanic Clouds, we can say at once that it must be an actual member of the distant cloud and not a neighbor of ours—not a member of the intervening foreground of stars contributed by our own system. The same attribution to

Fig. 18. The Bar of the Large Magellanic Cloud, R.A. 5^h 26^m, Dec. $-69°$.
(Harvard photograph, 10-inch telescope.)

Cloud membership is possible for the loose star clusters and the
gaseous nebulae found scattered over the Clouds. They do not belong to our own system because our loose clusters and gaseous
nebulae are very rarely found so far from the Milky Way.

The Loop Nebula, Star Clusters, and Peculiar Giant Stars

The most conspicuous of the gaseous nebulae of the Magellanic Clouds, and in fact one of the two or three most spectacular objects of its kind known anywhere in the sidereal world, is the Loop Nebula in the Large Cloud, which bears the constellation designation 30 Doradus. We reproduce in Fig. 19 a photograph of this enormous gaseous structure—a picture made with the 60-inch reflector at Harvard's southern station at Bloemfontein, in South Africa.

The distance to the large Magellanic Cloud is approximately 160,000 light-years (nearly a quintillion miles), and the linear diameter of the widely extended Loop Nebula is therefore astonishingly great. Let us compare it with the large nebula in Orion—a show object in our own Galaxy, about 1500 light-years distant. Both are visible to the unaided eye, the Orion Nebula appearing somewhat brighter. They have similar gaseous (bright-line) radiation; they are both associated with dense obscuring matter that conceals the stars lying beyond. They both have bright hot stars within them; and no doubt they owe to the high-temperature radiation of these included stars the energy that excites the gases to radiation. But the Orion Nebula is, in actual dimensions and in output of radiation, a pygmy compared with 30 Doradus. If the Loop Nebula were placed in the position of the Orion Nebula, it would fill the whole constellation of Orion, and the radiation from it and its involved supergiant stars would be strong enough to cast easily visible shadows on the earth. There is nothing like it in our own galactic system, as far as we can discover; but far away in some other galaxies we have found comparable supergiant gaseous nebulae.

Not until some special photographs were made in red light, thus removing the emphasis on the blue radiations that are characteristic of bright nebulosity, did we discover, in the center of 30 Doradus, a cluster of 100 or more supergiant stars, spreading over an irregularly bounded volume, approximately 200 light-years in diameter. This gigantic cluster of giants is about 400 times as bright intrinsically as the great globular cluster in Hercules. More justifiably than any other concentration of stars in the Large Cloud, it could claim to be the nucleus of the system, notwithstanding its somewhat eccentric location.

The Clouds of Magellan contain several globular clusters, and

Fig. 19. A detail of the preceding—the Great Loop Nebula as photographed at Bloemfontein with the Rockefeller telescope by J. S. Paraskevopoulos.

literally hundreds of open clusters of the Pleiades and Hyades types. Very little is as yet known about the globular clusters; their distance and compactness make them difficult objects to analyze. Long ago Miss Cannon found, as reported in the *Henry Draper Catalogue,* that the integrated light of many compact clusters is definitely blue (spectrum class *A*), not the typical yellow (spectra around *G*0) found for globular clusters associated with the Galaxy. This important result has been confirmed by others working with colors.

A considerable amount of attention has been devoted to the cataloguing and measuring of the open clusters in the Clouds. Much further research is in progress, especially at Cordoba in Argentina, Canberra in Australia, and the Boyden and Pretoria observatories in South Africa; the observers are mainly visiting astronomers from northern observatories. A descriptive catalogue of some 700 open clusters in the Large Cloud was made in 1959–60 by E. M. Lindsay and the present writer.

One special result obtained from the studies of the open clusters in the Magellanic Clouds should be reported, since it has a bearing on the investigations of the several hundred open clusters now known in our own Galaxy. It will be well, however, first to point out the most obvious advantage of using the Magellanic Clouds as an aid in the study of our own galactic organizations.

The Clouds contain, as mentioned above, many varieties of stars, nebulae, and clusters; and although so near that even moderate-sized telescopes can show the individual objects, yet they are sufficiently remote that we may treat them objectively. In this lies their high value. With them it is possible, in a sense, to escape from the troublesome effect of differing distances—a serious obstacle in the intercomparison of stars in our own Galaxy.

We can safely adopt the principle that all the stars in a Magellanic Cloud are at approximately the same distance from the earth. Then, if we find that the Cloud stars of some specific type *appear* to differ in brightness among themselves, we know that it is because they really do differ. If the apparent magnitudes in the Clouds range, on the photographic plate, from the tenth to the seventeenth, we can safely assume that the real luminosities of these stars also differ by seven magnitudes. It is otherwise in our galactic system.

To be sure, the Clouds have some thickness in the line of sight, and a star on the near side of the Cloud will be a bit brighter than if it were on the far edge; but the differences arising from location in the Cloud are small, relatively, and in our general analysis can be completely ignored. We can intercompare faint and bright stars in the Magellanic Clouds, knowing that we are intercomparing their candlepowers and not merely dealing with an illusion arising from conspicuously different distances, as is nearly always the circumstance when stars in our galactic system are intercompared.

Thus we may discover whether the peculiar class *O* stars in the Clouds are giants or supergiants in luminosity, or just average stars, because we can compare them directly with standard stars of known absolute luminosities, with the cepheids, for instance. The same procedure is possible for many other exotic objects that we should like to know about. The two Clouds turn out to be, therefore, a field in which to intercompare special or peculiar kinds of stars and nebulae. In pondering any particular evolutionary scheme, or development arrangement, we can now see quickly and certainly where a given object stands in the sequences of luminosities and masses; we can say responsibly whether it is perhaps a decadent star, or a primitive, or in mid-career.

We must as yet restrict our inquiries, however, to the candlepowers of giant and supergiant stars, because these nearby galaxies are so far away that no southern telescope yet constructed can photograph at their distances an ordinary star like our sun. We must deal chiefly with stars of from 10 to 10,000 times the luminosity of the sun, and solace ourselves with the reflection that most of the really interesting and active stars are giants of this sort. The sun and its kind are rather mediocre, and would be difficult to observe in detail from a distance greater than 50,000 light-years.

To return to the open clusters in the Large Magellanic Cloud, we note that we can take advantage of our outside viewpoint and usefully intercompare the dimensions of such clusters and the brightnesses of their luminous individual stars; and, in fact, intercompare their total luminosities. We can compare them also with the open clusters in our own galaxy—with the Pleiades and the Hyades.

In earlier work of my own on the clusters of the Milky Way, and subsequently in work by R. J. Trumpler of the Lick Observatory, it was found convenient to assume that the open clusters are of approximately identical dimensions wherever they occur, and, with less conviction, to assume that they are of similar integrated luminosities. That is, we assumed that the dispersions about the mean values of size and luminosity were not very great, and we hoped, therefore, that through measures of angular diameters, or of apparent magnitudes, we could deduce fair estimates of the distances to the scattered open clusters in our Galaxy. The method was simply a way to estimate distances to objects that are remote and extremely difficult to locate in space. It would have worked perfectly if clusters were identical, and if space were clear of dust and gas. We did not then know what the Magellanic Clouds had to say about the business. At the end of the next chapter we shall refer again to this method of distance estimation, and show that the full study and interpretation of the Magellanic Clouds may nevertheless aid in the better understanding of our own galactic system.

Many globular clusters of our Galaxy are rich in variable stars, especially rich in cluster variables. There is also in them a scattering of so-called "classical" cepheids. On the other hand, the open clusters of the Milky Way appear to have relatively few cepheids, or variables of any kind. This population difference is one of the distinguishing characteristics between the two main types of star clusters. But probably many of the cepheids in the variable-rich Magellanic Clouds are associated with the open clusters; and, thanks mostly to the recent work of J. B. Irwin, M. W. Feast, A. R. Sandage, R. P. Kraft, H. C. Arp, and S. van den Bergh, it is now known that several of the classical cepheids of the Milky Way are actually associated with open clusters of their neighborhoods. This is an important discovery since it aids in getting reliable values of the distances of some clusters and in making estimates of the amount of cosmic dust (space absorption) that partly obscures them. It will also lead to a check on the period-luminosity relation.

For one very rich open cluster of the Large Magellanic Cloud, namely, NGC 1866, Mrs. Nail and I in 1950 were able to show its association with a considerable number of classical cepheids. We determined their periods and light-curves, and found them to be typical of their class.

The Supergiant S Doradus

Before we leave the star clusters of the Large Magellanic Cloud, attention should be drawn to one irregular cluster that bears the catalogue number NGC 1910 (Fig. 20). It is nearly 400 light-years in diameter and contains a hundred or more giant and supergiant objects. One particular star, S Doradus, distinguishes this cluster, for it is possibly the most luminous star yet known in the whole universe, although to us, because of its distance of 160,000 light-years, it is considerably below naked-eye brightness. S Doradus is a variable star of an unusual sort, irregular in its light variations and of the peculiar P Cygni type of spectrum. With a light fluctuation from magnitude 8.2 to 9.4, its luminosity averages about 1,000,000 times that of the sun. It must certainly be a giant in size also, probably exceeding the orbit of the earth in diameter. Sergei Gaposchkin has suggested that the star is actually double, with the equal components periodically eclipsing each other in a cycle of 40 years.

S Doradus is no doubt a blue, hot, highly efficient radiator (or pair of radiators). The many reddish supergiant stars distributed throughout the Cloud give out nearly as much radiation, but, since they are relatively inefficient radiators, their diameters must in some instances be much greater—equal to that of the orbit of Jupiter—in order to provide sufficient radiative surface to maintain the enormous output of energy we observe. It is quite probable that in size many of these red giants in the Magellanic Clouds considerably exceed the greatest of the naked-eye stars near the sun, being bigger even than Antares and Betelgeuse. Certainly they much exceed those two stars in total radiation.

Possibly S Doradus was once a supernova, and, notwithstanding its excessive output of radiation, has failed to fade toward obscurity during the 70 years it has been under observation. Some ordinary novae are also slow about fading away after their explosive appearances. But a double supernova! That picture is hard to see.

Fig. 20. S Doradus, a supergiant variable described in the text, is at the center of the circle in the loose clustering called NGC 1910. Two of the Large Magellanic Cloud's globular clusters are shown in the lower part of the figure. (Harvard photograph, Rockefeller telescope.)

Distances and Dimensions

With the aid of the variable stars, as described in the next chapter, we have been able to determine the distance of the Magellanic Clouds as 160,000 light-years. There is some uncertainty in the allowance we have made for light-absorbing gas and dust in our own Milky Way. This interstellar material cuts down the brightness of objects seen through it so that they appear to be fainter (and more distant) than they would be in a dust-free sky. The amount of dimming estimated for the Clouds on the basis of a census of the galaxies in the background is 0.4 magnitude.

The Clouds are separated, center from center, by 21°, which corresponds roughly to 60,000 light-years. The distance from border to border is not more than the diameter of the Large Cloud. We can fairly propose that the two objects form a double system, faintly acting on each other gravitationally.

Actually the edges of the two Clouds are much closer together than they appear to be on first inspection. Special photographic plates, and a detailed counting of the faint stars, as well as diligent searching for outlying variables and open clusters, have greatly extended the recognized boundaries of both systems. In fact, each Cloud now appears to be a concentrated irregular mass of stars surrounded by a lightly populated envelope. That is, a haze of stars apparently surrounds the main body, which contains most of the mass of the system. Baade finds a similar corona of faint stars around the irregular dwarf galaxy IC 1613 (see Chapter 5). The extent to which the boundaries of the Clouds have been pushed by the investigations carried on at the Harvard Observatory is indicated in Fig. 21. Evidence has been advanced by G. de Vaucouleurs, and by Frank Kerr and associates, using a radio telescope, to support the view that the Clouds are much flattened, and tilted from the line of sight by 30° for the Small Cloud and 65° for the Large—a suggestion that future radial-velocity work can test. The enveloping star haze is probably little flattened.

The extension in size of the Small Magellanic Cloud was first revealed on small-scale photographs of long exposure. The plates were made 50 years ago at an exploratory testing site in South Africa; some have exposures in excess of 20 hours. An extension, or wing, as indicated in Fig. 21, is directed toward the Large Cloud. It shows that the two systems may be nearly in contact by way of this faint stellar bridge. Within a few years we may be able to show that the star hazes of the Magellanic Clouds overlap—that the Clouds are, in a sense, two massive irregular nuclei in an over-all stellar envelope.

The recent work in Australia by Kerr and associates indicates that a hydrogen-gas envelope surrounds and permeates both Clouds, so

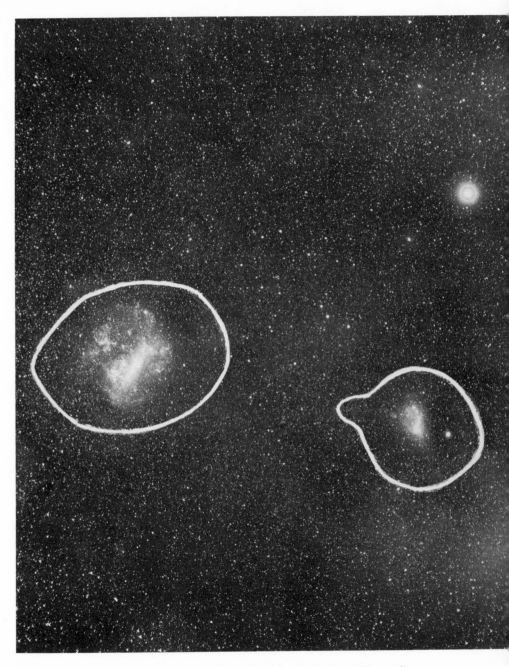

Fig. 21. The overflow areas of the Magellanic Clouds, and the wing of the smaller. The bright star Achernar is also on the photograph. (Harvard photograph, AX camera.)

that, even if we discover no stellar connectant, a bridge of inter-galactic gas is now indicated. It seems certain that both of these external galaxies lie within or at the edge of the star haze of our own galactic system. Their distances from the galactic plane are approximately 90,000 light-years for the Large Cloud and 110,000 for the Small. Some of our Galaxy's globular clusters and cluster-type cepheid variables are nearly as distant from the plane. One might consider the Clouds to be satellites of our much larger Galaxy; and certainly they are within its effective gravitational domain. These points are to be considered further in Chapter 5 when we examine the other neighbors of the Milky Way.

On the Future of the Clouds

One is tempted to ask, without hope of an immediate answer, what has been the past career of these two ragged galaxies that are so near our dominating galactic system; what is to be their immediate future (in the next billion years), and their ultimate fate as units in the Metagalaxy? Are they escaping from us, or coming in, or just tagging along? The partial answers now advanced help but little. No cross motions are as yet certainly detectable. W. J. Luyten, using Harvard photographs, has shown that the cross motions must be exceedingly small.

The motions in the line of sight have been measured by R. E. Wilson with spectrograms from the southern station of the Lick Observatory, and more recently at Pretoria and by the Australian radio astronomers. The Large Cloud recedes from the earth with a speed of about 170 miles per second, and the Small Cloud, which is further from the galactic plane, with a speed of about 100 miles per second. But these figures represent chiefly our own rapid motion in our rotating Galaxy. They give the speed of our rotation about the nucleus in Sagittarius. Allowing for the rotational motion, we find that the line-of-sight speeds of the Large and Small Cloud in miles per second are about 0 and +50, respectively. Improved values of the speeds should soon be available from the radio and optical telescopes. We shall need more accurate measures of the radial velocity to be able to say certainly that the Small Cloud is now moving away. It would help our interpretation if we had measures also of the cross motions. In the course of a century or two that component of the motions should be known with some accuracy.

3

The Astronomical Toolhouse

The two Clouds of Magellan, as remarked in the preceding chapter, are satisfactorily located in space for the effective study of many properties of galaxies, even though inconveniently far south for easy exploitation by the majority of astronomers. Their distance of about 160,000 light-years gives easy access to all of their giant and supergiant stars. Their considerable angular separations from the star clouds of the Milky Way keep them clear not only of most of the light-scattering dust near the galactic plane, but also of the confusingly rich foreground of stars and nebulosity near the Milky Way. They are nicely isolated.

During the past half century high profit has accrued from our studies of these nearby gal-

axies, for they have turned out to be veritable treasure chests of
sidereal knowledge, and astronomical toolhouses of great merit. We
shall see that the hypotheses, deductions, and techniques that arise
from studies of the stars and nebulae of the Magellanic galaxies can
be used to explore our own surrounding system, and also the more
distant galaxies.

The usefulness of the Magellanic Clouds in the larger problems
of cosmography can be illustrated by presenting, without stopping
now to explain the meaning of the items or their significance, a
partial list of the contributions of our knowledge of stars and galaxies
that have already come from studies of the Clouds, or are on the
way:

1. The period-luminosity relation;
2. The general luminosity curve, that is, the relative number of
stars in successive intervals of intrinsic brightness;
3. Measures of the internal motions of irregular galaxies;
4. A comparison of the sizes, luminosities, and types of open
star clusters;
5. The frequency of cepheid variation, shown by the number of
cepheid variables compared with the numbers of other types of
giant stars of approximately the same mass and brightness;
6. The spread of the period lengths of cepheid variables;
7. The dependence of various characteristics of the light curve
of cepheid variables on the length of period;
8. The dependence of a cepheid's period on location in a galaxy;
9. The total absolute magnitudes of globular star clusters, and
the maximum luminosity of numerous special types of stars;
10. The demonstration of the "star haze" and "hydrogen haze"
surrounding some if not all galaxies.

It seems inevitable that additional discoveries will reward the
future investigators of these two external systems that can be studied
objectively and in detail because of their nearness and externality.

Nearly all of the subjects listed can be investigated more successfully in the Magellanic Clouds than elsewhere. And many can be
read about in the technical reports better than here. Some involve
the problems of stellar evolution; others, of galactic dimensions and
structure. Several of the items will have their use chiefly in the
future, rather than in the past; and although all are important in
astronomy, only a few can be considered fully in this chapter.

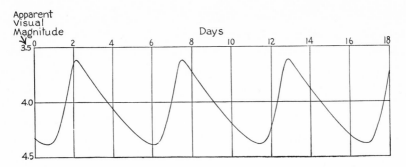

Fig. 22. An 18-day section of the light curve of the typical cepheid variable Delta Cephei, which for indefinite centuries will faithfully and monotonously repeat the 5.37-day oscillation.

The Abundance of Cepheid Variables

The outstanding phenomenon associated with the Magellanic Clouds is undoubtedly the relatively great number of giant variable stars, of which a majority are of the cepheid class (Fig. 22). They are easily available for detailed investigation since they stand out conspicuously among the brighter stars. Practically all the 2500 "classical" cepheid variables in the Magellanic Clouds are shown on good 1-hour photographs made with the Bruce telescope or its successor the ADH Schmidt reflector at Bloemfontein, but this does not include cluster cepheids with periods of less than a day.

In each of the Clouds there are more classical cepheid variables than are as yet known in our own much larger galaxy. The survey in the Clouds approaches completeness; the survey in the galactic system is fragmentary and seriously hindered by the interstellar dust along the Milky Way where classical cepheids are concentrated. Probably fewer than half of the cepheid variables of our Milky Way system have been detected.

Of the variable stars in the Magellanic Clouds that have been worked up, about 80 percent are classical cepheids. In the neighborhood of the sun there are only a few of these pulsating stars; among them are Polaris and Delta Cephei, the latter being the star that gives a name to the class. In the solar neighborhood, as elsewhere in the galactic system, variables of other types are considerably more numerous than cepheids; for instance, here there are hundreds of eclipsing binaries, whereas only a few score are known in the Magellanic Clouds. Also we have found in our Galaxy more than

3000 "cluster" variables, which are the cepheid variables with periods less than a day, but not one had been identified with certainty in the Magellanic Clouds until recently when the large reflector of the Radcliffe Observatory at Pretoria revealed faintly some of these objects in the Large Cloud's globular clusters. In the galactic system there are a great many long-period variables—the kind of stars that are carefully watched by the organized variable-star observers—but such stars are not yet abundant in the records of the Clouds.

Does this richness in the Magellanic Clouds of classical cepheid variables, with periods between 1 and 50 days, indicate that the population differs fundamentally in such irregular galaxies from that in the Milky Way spiral? Not necessarily so. The relative scarcity of cluster-type cepheids, long-period variables, and eclipsing stars in the present records of the Clouds is best accounted for by the relatively low candlepower of variable stars of those types. Even at maximum, such variables are not quite bright enough to get numerously into our eighteenth-magnitude picture of the Magellanic Clouds. Until recently we have photographed almost exclusively the giants that are 200 times or more brighter than the sun. The larger reflectors are beginning to explore among the fainter stars and possibly will soon reveal many cluster variables at the nineteenth magnitude, and eventually get down to stars of the sun's brightness.

The Period-Luminosity Relation

Some years after Miss Leavitt had discovered and published 1777 variable stars in the two Clouds, she presented the results of a study of the periods of some of the variables. For the investigation she had selected the brightest of the variables as well as a few fainter ones. At once there appeared the interesting fact that, when the average brightness of a given variable is high, the period, which is the time interval separating successive maxima of brightness, is long compared with the intervals for fainter stars. The fainter the variable, the shorter the period.

The graph of her results for 25 variables is reproduced in Fig. 23. It is of historic significance. Miss Leavitt and Professor Pickering recognized at once that if the periods of variation depend on the brightness they must also be associated with other physical char-

Magnitude

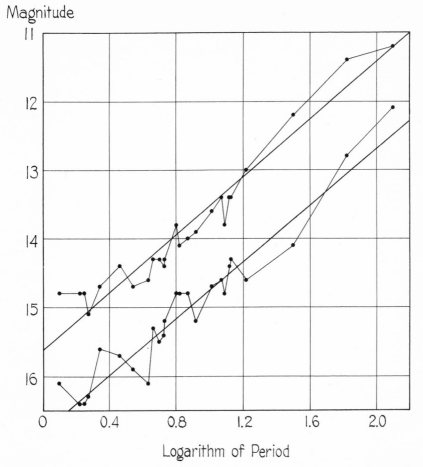

Logarithm of Period

Fig. 23.   Miss Leavitt's original diagram showing, separately for the maxima and the minima of 25 variable stars in the Small Cloud, the relation between photographic magnitude (vertical ordinate) and the logarithm of the period (horizontal ordinate).

acteristics of the stars, such as mass and density and size. But apparently they did not foresee that this relation between brightness and period for cepheids in the Small Cloud would be the preliminary blueprint of one of astronomy's most potent tools for measuring the universe; not did they, in fact, identify these variables of the Magellanic Cloud with the already well-known cepheid variables of the solar neighborhood. They simply had found a curiosity among the variables of the Small Magellanic Cloud.

Soon after Miss Leavitt's announcement of the period-magnitude

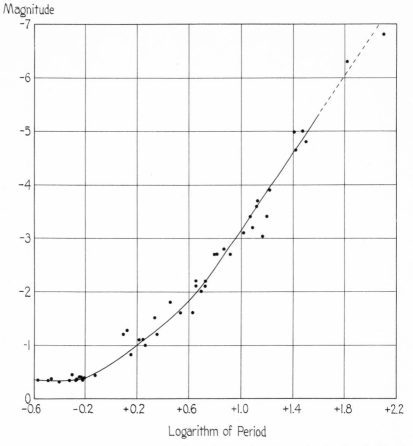

Fig. 24. The early period-luminosity relation, based on the 25 Small Cloud variables and cepheids from the globular clusters and the galactic system. The ordinates here are visual magnitudes on the absolute scale. (The curve has been revised since 1952, with the variables in globular clusters separated from those of the Clouds.)

relation for this small fraction of the variables that she had discovered in the Small Magellanic Cloud, Ejnar Hertzsprung and others pointed out that the nearby cepheid variable stars of the Milky Way are giants—a fact that was readily deduced from their small cross motions and from spectral peculiarities. Therefore, if the galactic cepheids and the Magellanic variables are closely comparable in luminosities, these fifteenth- and sixteenth-magnitude objects in the Clouds must also be giants; and in order to appear so faint, they must be very remote, and so also must be the Clouds.

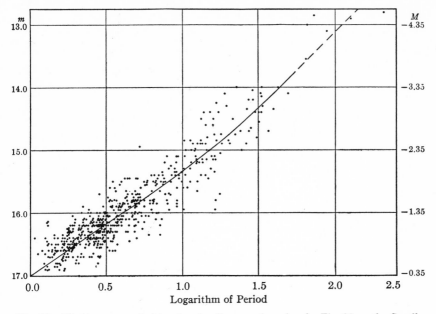

Fig. 25. The present period-luminosity diagram, based as for Fig. 23 on the Small Cloud alone. Both apparent and absolute (photographic) magnitudes are indicated; the absolute magnitudes M are referred to the 1953 revision of the zero point. The scattering of the points about the curve is of much significance.

I and others pursued the inquiry and supplemented Miss Leavitt's work by studies of the variable stars that Bailey and others had detected in the globular star clusters. The many variables of the globular clusters are mostly cepheids of the cluster type with periods less than a day. But also in clusters are a few longer-period cepheids, and it was eventually possible to bring together all the data necessary for a practical but tentative period-luminosity curve. The new investigation appeared to connect the typical or "classical" cepheids with the cluster variables. I then derived a zero point from trigonometric measures of the distances of the nearby cepheids and thereby changed the Leavitt relation from period and *apparent* magnitude to period and *absolute* luminosity, thus making distances determinable from light measures only, as will be shown below. My first (1917) period-luminosity curve is reproduced in Fig. 24, and in Fig. 25 is the revised (1942) edition of the most essential part of the curve. The latter is based on homogeneous material, free of the variables in globular clusters and in the Milky Way.

The period-luminosity curve of 1917 depended on only 25 Small Cloud variables and a limited assemblage of cepheids from the galactic system and from various globular clusters, but the 1942 revision was based on 564 variables in the Small Cloud; it required some 40,000 estimates of magnitude, as well as the establishment of homogeneous magnitude standards throughout the Cloud.

There never has been much doubt about the general form of the period-luminosity curve, but its zero point, the true absolute magnitude M for a given period, has frequently been in question. I made a small adjustment of the original value soon after the curve was first set up.

Extensive early studies of the zero point, chiefly by R. E. Wilson working on neighboring cepheids, indicated that all is well, or at least temporarily satisfactory, so far as it concerns variable stars in globular clusters and cluster variables wherever found. Their median absolute magnitudes are probably near zero, with an uncertainty, however, of two or three tenths of a magnitude, or even more.

But it is quite different with the classical cepheids (periods greater than 1 day), for Baade and others have now shown that there are two kinds of classical cepheids and they both have period-luminosity relations. The classical cepheids in the Magellanic Clouds apparently are about 1.5 magnitudes (absolute) brighter at a given period than those associated with globular clusters. (Our Milky Way has both types.) The classical cepheids in the Magellanic Clouds are therefore truly gigantic, and, since they appear faint (magnitudes mostly 14 to 16), their revised distances must be substantially greater than computed with the period-luminosity relation in Fig. 24.

The zero point was therefore adjusted a second time in 1955. The correction, which amounts to doubling the distances of the Magellanic Clouds, affects also the computation of the distances of the other external galaxies, and therefore affects the calculation of the speed of the expansion of the universe—a subject that is treated in the final chapter of this volume. Once we have decided on the zero point of the period-luminosity graph in Fig. 25, we can use that graph to determine the distances of all those external systems that contain measured classical cepheids. Since even now the zero point is not firmly fixed, our measures of distances in the Metagalaxy may remain "rough" for many years.

This matter of zero point is of much importance, because it sets the absolute scale of distances of all galaxies. Without a secure zero point, only relative distances can be obtained through the use of cepheids. Other objects, like common novae, can eventually be used in estimating distances of galaxies, but the standardization again is based on the zero point of cepheids. The reliability of all the great distances to which cosmogonists now refer is essentially dependent on our derivation of correct candlepowers (luminosities) of the cepheid variables within a few hundred light-years of the sun. And the luminosities of these nearby cepheids that fix the zero point are determined, it should be noted, almost exclusively by the methods of what is now called the old-fashioned astronomy—by the accurate measurement, that is, of the positions, "trigonometric" distances, and proper motions of the local cepheids. To the extent that the distances of these critical stars are uncertain, the zero point is uncertain; also uncertain in consequence are the distances of the Magellanic Clouds and of other galaxies, and the size of the measurable universe. Hence the importance of more work on the distances and luminosities of bright nearby cepheids like Polaris and Delta Cephei.

It may be well at this point to show how one uses the period-luminosity curve of Fig. 25 to measure the distances of the classical cepheids in our Milky Way, or the distance to some remote external galaxy, like the Andromeda Nebula. The procedure is very simple, once the period-luminosity relation is set up and accurately calibrated. First must come the discovery of a periodic variable star, and then, through the making of a hundred or so observations of the brightness at scattered times, comes the verification, from the shape of the mean light curve, that the variable belongs to the cepheid class. On a correct magnitude scale we next determine the amplitude (range) of variation, and the value of the magnitude half-way between maximum and minimum. This *median apparent magnitude,* $\dot{m}$, which is now almost always determined photographically rather than visually, constitutes one half of the needed observational material. The other half, namely the period P, is also determined from the observations of magnitudes.

With the period and its logarithm known, the relative absolute luminosity, $\dot{M}$, is then derived directly from Fig. 25, or from a table or formula based on the mean curve of Fig. 25. For example, the simple formula

$$\dot{M} = -1.78 - 1.74 \log P$$

is satisfactory for getting the relative absolute magnitudes of all cepheids with periods between 1.2 and 40 days.

When we have thus derived the relative absolute magnitude from the period, we compute the distance d from the equally simple relation

$$\log d = 0.2 \, (\dot{m} - \dot{M} - \delta m) + 1,$$

where the distance is expressed in parsecs (1 parsec = 3.26 light-years, or about 19 trillion miles), and δm is the correction one must make to the observed median magnitude because of the scattering and absorption of starlight by the dust and gas of interstellar space. (The derivation of this standard formula is given by Bart J. Bok and Priscilla F. Bok in *The Milky Way,* and in various general textbooks.)

If space is essentially transparent, as in directions toward the poles of the Galaxy, δm can be set equal to zero. Such is the case for Messier 3 (Fig. 26). In directions where scattering is appreciable, we are frequently in trouble because δm is not zero and is difficult to determine. When we ignore the correction we have an upper limit for the distance. Thus, for cepheids in the Milky Way star clouds, where there is much dimming from dust, we can from this simple procedure, when scattering is ignored, determine only that the cepheids are not more remote than the computed distance; if δm is 1.5 magnitudes, they are actually only half as distant.

For a cepheid in a galaxy well away from the dust-filled Milky Way star clouds, we can safely assume that δm is less than 0.3, and rather accurately compute the distance of the cepheid from the formulas above. We then have not only the distance of the cepheid, whose $\dot{M}$ we get from P and whose $\dot{m}$ and P we get from the measures of magnitude, but also, without further measurement, we have the distance of the whole galaxy of a thousand million stars or more.

In summary, this simple but powerful photometric method based on cepheid variables involves only the observational determination of the periods and apparent magnitudes, followed by a direct calculation of absolute magnitudes and distances; we assume that our cepheid is of the Magellanic type and not of the aberrant type found in some globular clusters.

Since cepheids with median photographic magnitudes as faint as the nineteenth can be discovered and studied with several existing telescopes, and since such cepheids may have periods of 40 days,

Fig. 26. The globular cluster Messier 3, one of the most conspicuous in the northern sky, is renowned for its nearly 200 cluster-type cepheids that have been intensively studied in half a dozen countries by S. I. Bailey, E. E. Barnard, J. L. Greenstein, P. Guthnick, F. Larink, G. R. Miczaika, Th. Müller, H. B. Sawyer, M. Schwarzschild, H. Shapley, P. Slavenas, H. von Zeipel, and others. (Palomar photograph, 200-inch telescope.)

we can with the period-luminosity relation readily measure enormous distances. For example, a period of 40 days gives

$$\dot{M} = -1.78 - 1.74 \times 1.60 = -4.56$$

according to the first formula above. Then, away from the Milky Way absorption, the second formula gives

$$\log d = 0.2(19.0 + 4.56) + 1 = 5.712.$$

The distance that is measurable with this supergiant cepheid in high latitudes is therefore $d = 520,000$ parsecs, or approximately 1,700,000 light-years. The uncertainty in the result, on a percentage basis, is distinctly less than that in a measurement locally of 500 light-years by the older trigonometric method.

How Many of the Giant Stars Are Cepheids?

The 800 variable stars found in Miss Leavitt's early survey of the Large Cloud of Magellan are well distributed throughout the structure as ordinarily seen and photographed, and several were found beyond the easily recognized boundaries. The photographs available for her study were not numerous. Many years later, with new photographs, it was possible to reexamine this galaxy and provide more completely a census of its cepheids. The later Harvard abservers have increased the number of known variables to about 1400, making some 20,000 estimates of magnitude in the process of confirming the reality of the variations. All of these objects, and about 150 additional stars strongly suspected of being variable, are plotted in Fig. 27 in a special diagram that is intended to suggest the main structural features of the Cloud. This cosmographic figure may be compared directly with the photograph of the Cloud in Fig. 28.

It is now known, as suggested in Fig. 21, that the Cloud actually extends far beyond the sketched-in boundaries of Fig. 27. The main body of the system, however, lies within the plotted boundary, which also encloses a large proportion of the discovered variable stars. From the photograph it is seen that there is a dominating "bar" in the center of the Cloud, outlined in the diagram with the heavy continuous line. Regions rich in clustering are indicated with lighter continuous borders, and other regions, bounded with broken lines, are intermediate between these rich clustered areas and the general open fields of the Cloud. In examining the photo-graph, and noting how the variable stars are distributed through-out these various regions, we must remember that some thousands of intervening stars of our own system are projected against the background of the Cloud.

In the examination of variable-star distribution we have a chance to do something that only with great difficulty could be accomplished in our own galactic system. We can find the frequency of cepheid variables relative to the invariable stars. We find that about 2 percent of all the supergiants in the Large Cloud between the thirteenth and sixteenth photographic magnitudes are cepheids. The proportion varies throughout the Cloud structure, rising to about 4 percent along the central bar and falling to less than 0.5 percent in the sparsely populated areas. This concentration of cepheids to the more populous regions is similar to the conspicuous concentration of classical cepheids in our own system to the stellar regions along the Milky Way.

What Period Is Most Frequent?

After several years of persistent study of the Magellanic variables, we are now able to examine with positive results both the distribution of cepheids throughout a stellar system and the relative frequencies of their periods. We use the data available from the Small Cloud, where the periods of 670 variables are now known, and look first to see if the period-luminosity curve varies in shape or in zero point from one section to another. The curve, for some unknown reason, might be steeper at the edges of the Cloud than at the center, or in one part of the Cloud the scattering and absorbing material might dim all the stellar magnitudes, depressing the zero point, while in other sections the Cloud might be wholly free from such dimming. We had rather hoped, in fact, while carrying on this investigation, to find evidence here and there of measurable differences in the zero point of the period-luminosity curve, differences to which we could point as providing a good method for measuring the amount of dimming produced by dust particles and gas in a galactic system. But no appreciable differences have been found. The zero point and the slope of the period-luminosity curve are the same in the dense regions as in the thinly populated outer fields. If there is such space absorption inside the Small Magellanic Cloud,

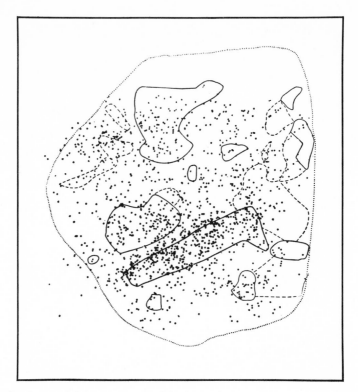

Fig. 27. A superficial cosmograph of the Large Cloud with the position of cepheid variables indicated. The upper part of the Cloud has not yet been examined thoroughly for stellar variation.

it must on the average be pretty small, or be evenly distributed and not concentrated to the periphery or to the regions of high star density.

In studies of the Small Cloud variables by the writer, with the assistance of Mrs. Virginia McK. Nail, an unexpected relation did, however, come to light, and we are still ignorant of what the discovery means. In fact, we appear to have made a double contribution to the increasing knowledge of cepheid variables, which continue to stand out as the most important kind of star known to the astronomers.

In the first place, we found that the partial census of cepheid variables in our galaxy had apparently led us to an erroneous idea of the frequency distribution of the periods. For many years we had tacitly assumed that the distribution of the periods is actually as

Fig. 28. The Large Cloud photographed on the same scale as the cosmograph on the opposite page. In both figures the bar can be recognized, and also the cluster-full regions, and the wide open spaces. See also Fig. 18. (Harvard photograph, Bache telescope.)

shown in Fig 29, which represented all the data available in 1942 for the classical cepheids in the galactic system. The curve shows that the most frequent period is between 4 and 5 days. A decided scarcity of periods is noted between 1.0 and 2.5 days, and also a minimum in the frequency curve at about 9 days, with secondary maxima, perhaps, at 10 and 16 days.

The preliminary survey of the distribution of periods in the Small Magellanic Cloud gave very similar results. We seemed to have in this form of the frequency curve a "rule of nature." But it turns out that because of our eccentrically located observing station in our own galactic system, and because of its great size and its troublesome dustiness, we had a very incomplete census of galactic cepheids and an imperfect knowledge of the distribution of their

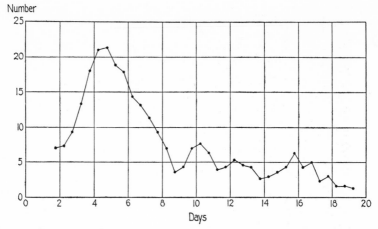

Fig. 29.   Frequency of periods of known cepheid variables in the galactic system (as of 1942). The few cepheids with periods longer than 20 days, and the many cluster-type cepheids with periods less than 1 day, are not plotted.

periods. It appears also that the first hundred variable stars for which periods were measured in the Small Magellanic Cloud were so selected that here too we had an unfinished picture.

To rectify matters, it was only necessary to determine the periods for *all* the discoverable cepheids in some well-distributed regions of the Small Cloud, and thus procure, through a large and fair sampling, a true picture of the frequency distribution of periods. It turns out to be as shown in Fig. 30, in which the full line represents the distribution of periods in the Small Cloud, and the broken line, adapted from Fig. 29, shows the course of the frequency curve for galactic cepheids. This true, or nearly true, curve of period distribution in the Cloud shows a maximum near 2 days where previously there was a minimum; it shows no minimum at 9 days or maximum at 10 days.

Perhaps we are overemphasizing the importance of the distribution of periods. But certainly the cepheid variable star, with its periodically changing light, size, and temperature, is of continual importance as a cosmic laboratory. Some of our theoretical investigations of stellar structure and of the release mechanism of stellar radiation are bound up with the periods and the modes of cepheid vibrations. Now we know that the most frequent period for cepheid variables in the Small Cloud is 2 or 3 days shorter than presumed from earlier studies, and therefore the most frequent values of the

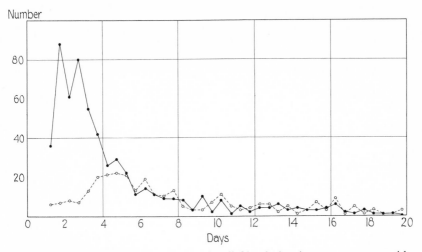

Fig. 30. The period distribution in the Small Cloud, showing great contrast with the distribution for the galactic system, which is represented by a broken line and open circles.

density, size, and surface temperature are other than we had supposed. Polaris, with a period of 3.97 days, and Delta Cephei, with a period of 5.37 days, are not average the whole world over.

The situation, however, may be more complicated than now appears. In the Large Magellanic Cloud, where 550 periods of cepheids have been derived, only 1 percent are shorter than 2.1 days; for the Small Cloud, 24 percent of 670 periods are shorter than 2.1 days. The research should proceed to a definitive test of this remarkable result. Most other external galaxies unfortunately are so distant that their fainter, more rapidly pulsating variables are still beyond our telescopic power.

At any rate, our astronomical treasure chest has yielded one more interesting item, which may eventually be a usable tool for probing the interiors of stars.

An Indicator of Gravitational Potential, or Something

The second interesting outcome of our examination of the period distribution is the discovery that *on the average* the cepheid variables in the regions of high star density have decidedly longer periods than those in the outlying rarer regions. Fig. 31 illustrates the difference clearly. The full line refers to completely surveyed regions

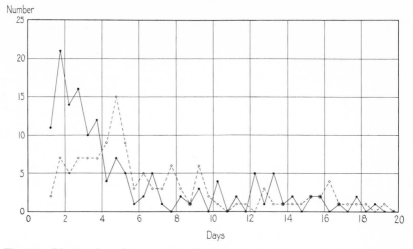

Fig. 31. Distribution of the periods of cepheids in the inner and outer regions of the Small Cloud. The broken line represents the former.

at the edges of the Small Cloud, out where one can hardly recognize what is star cloud and what is intervening star field of the galactic system. In these outer regions very short periods predominate. The broken line shows the distribution of periods for the fully explored innermost regions, that is, for the main body of the Cloud; there shorter periods are scare. That such conspicuous differences in average period should exist is surprising, because they indicate correspondingly large differences in the average mass and candlepower of the variables. They suggest that the earlier history of this stellar system is being revealed by the characteristics of the cepheids, but we do not yet know how to read the records.

Perhaps the relative abundance of the various chemical elements in the hypothetical prestar state of the Small Cloud varied from massive center to the boundaries; and it is probable that the masses and sizes of stars, and the speeds of their evolution, depend on the elemental composition of the stuff from which they condense. This view can be sensibly argued now that star age and atomic composition are thought to be linked.

Or perhaps the universe is very old, and the earlier dynamic experiences of stars in the Small Magellanic Cloud were vigorous, the motions turbulent. In that event the less massive short-period cepheids were cast out into the border regions as a result of encounters with the more massive nuclear stars, including the long-period cepheids. Said otherwise, perhaps the present peculiar distribution reflects the operation of the principle of equipartition of energy. That process would require much time.

Or more likely there is some happier interpretation, since neither of these hypotheses is appealing. Obviously we shall be better prepared to speculate on this phenomenon after we have strengthened the observational basis by determining the positions, periods, and median magnitudes of the several hundred other cepheid variables in the Small Cloud, and after we have explored more deeply the Large Cloud's contribution to the question of variable-star distribution. The preliminary surveys give for it a less pronounced correlation of period length with star density. In our own system there is also evidence that the massive long-period cepheids show an affinity for the rich nucleus of the Galaxy. Whether astrochemistry or galactic dynamics is responsible for what we observe in the Small Cloud, we can again record that an astronomical tool of peculiar significance may be in the making.

The Light Curves of Cepheids

If the candlepower is closely related to the period for a cepheid variable, is it not likely that other characteristics of the light variation also depend on the period? Several years ago, working with galactic cepheids, Hertzsprung produced some evidence of a progressive change in the shape of the average light curve with period. The light curves for stars with periods around 10 days were found to be generally symmetric, while light curves for stars with periods of from 15 to 20 days showed greater amplitudes and were decidedly asymmetric.

The comparative study of the light curves of cepheids in the Milky Way, such as that carried out by Hertzsprung, suffers from the many difficulties associated with photographic photometry. Especially difficult is the discriminating comparison of one variable with another when they are widely separated. The intercomparisons can be much more comfortably made in the Magellanic Clouds, where the cepheids of various periods are near together, all on the same photographic plates, and all readily studied with the use of a single set of standard reference stars.

Figure 32 illustrates a short series of carefully evaluated curves. The ordinates and abscissas, as usual, are apparent magnitude and

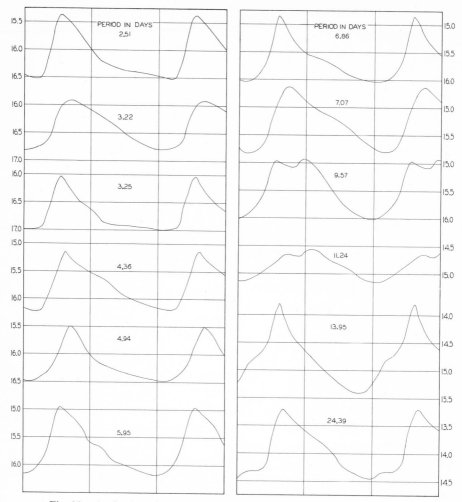

Fig. 32. A selection of cepheid light curves from the Large Cloud, to illustrate both the variety of curves and the peculiar form for the light curves when the periods are in the vicinity of 10 days. The horizontal scale, as usual, is in terms of time.

time (phase), with all the time scales adjusted in such a way that the light curves have the same horizontal length, whether the periods are short or long. Some variety appears in the light curves at any given period, and our derivation of ten times as many accurate light curves supports this evidence of variety. The cepheids, therefore, seem to have personalities of their own. There is on the average, however, a progressive pattern. (We may also read in the margin of this diagram that the longer the period, the brighter the star; it holds at maximum, at minimum, and at median magnitude. This progression of brightness with period is, of course, merely the well-known period-luminosity relation.)

The individuality of the cepheids is further illustrated in Fig. 33, where six stars of almost exactly the same period are shown to differ remarkably in magnitude, although they are, of course, at essentially the same distance. Two are brighter and three are much fainter than average. Is this difference in luminosity real, or only apparent? The brighter objects may, of course, be on the nearer edge of the Cloud and the fainter ones on the far edge, but that could account for only a small portion of the observed deviation. It may be that the three fainter objects are dimmed by obscuration (dust and gas) within the Small Cloud.

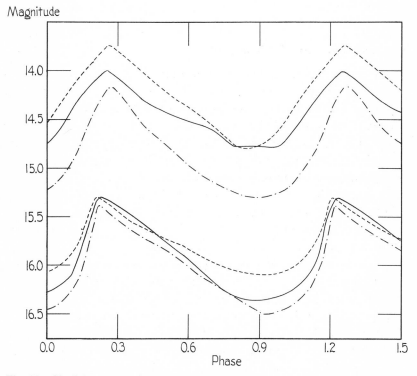

Fig. 33. Six light curves of variables in the Small Cloud, to illustrate the effect of light absorption and possibly other factors. The periods of the six stars differ but little from 16.5 days. By the period-luminosity relation one would expect the light curves to be nearly superimposed, but three of the stars are abnormally faint for some reason, and two are brighter than normal.

Other factors may contribute to the scatter of individual values around the mean period-luminosity curve—a scatter best shown by the spread of points in the period-luminosity graph of Fig. 25. A close examination of oppositely diverging values seems to show, however, that there is a real spread among the cepheids of a given period. The period-luminosity relation is an average relation, not unique and absolute; a given period does not precisely demand one definite value of candlepower. We are therefore the victims of an inescapable source of error—of an error that may frequently amount to 20 percent or more in the distance of an individual isolated cepheid, or of an external galaxy if its estimated distance depends on a single cepheid. For estimating the distance of a galaxy it will generally be possible to use several cepheids, so that in the mean the effect of scatter is canceled, or at least much diminished.

The Luminosity Curve for Supergiants

After a census is made of a community of people or of stars, it is often of interest to know how the sizes or weights or brightnesses are distributed—how many individuals there are, for instance, of the various recorded diameters. A graph shows the distribution most plainly. The numbers of stars of a given type in successive intervals of absolute magnitude, plotted against the absolute magnitudes, is commonly called the *luminosity curve* for such stars. The luminosity curve may have one form for cepheid variables (featuring few supergiants, a great many giants, and no average or dwarf representatives), and a quite different shape for the red giant stars of the class of Antares and Betelgeuse.

The *general luminosity curve* lumps all types together. It is simply the frequency curve of the absolute magnitudes of all stars in a stellar system for which one does not bother to discriminate among types, or is unable to discriminate among them. It has a limited usefulness in the general study of stellar evolution; but since there is for a majority of stars a fundamental relation between the mass of a star and its present luminosity (absolute magnitude), the general luminosity curve of a stellar system does yield some significant information on the frequency of individual masses and on the total mass of a stellar organization.

One of the more stubborn problems in the astronomy of our own

Milky Way has been the derivation and analysis of the general luminosity curve. Because of our immersion deep in our own stellar system, we have difficulty in formulating a wholesome view of the Galaxy. We are bothered by natural preferences for nearby stars, or for highly luminous objects that are impressive though remote. And we are most bedeviled by the obnoxious gas and dust that foul interstellar space and mislead our measures of magnitude and distance.

The problem, however, can be attacked without these handicaps in an outside system like the Magellanic Clouds. We can there be sure, as we are not sure at home, that our survey of stars down to a given magnitude is complete. But the surety holds only for the supergiant and giant stars, because we are not yet able, with Boyden Observatory equipment (Fig. 34) or other southern telescopes, to reach effectively to the fainter objects, for example, to stars of the sun's brightness. In the Magellanic Clouds our luminosity curves extend, as shown in Fig. 35 for the Large Cloud, from the brightest supergiants, more than 100,000 times the solar brightness, to star about 100 times as bright as the sun. In the near future the surveys will go much fainter, at least in special regions in the Clouds.

The census of the highly luminous stars has been made by counting in sample areas scattered throughout the Cloud. The areas are selected so as to give a fair representation of the very unevenly disposed population. The results are indicative rather than accurate; but they permit the construction of Table 1, which illustrates the

TABLE 1.   *A preliminary census of supergiant and giant stars in the Large Magellanic Cloud.*

Absolute photographic magnitude	Total number of stars
Brighter than −6.5	735
−6.5 to −6.0	940
−6.0 to −5.5	1,460
−5.5 to −5.0	2,400
−5.0 to −4.5	3,260
−4.5 to −4.0	6,830
−4.0 to −3.5	11,080
−3.5 to −3.0	16,080
−3.0 to −2.5	23,170
−2.5 to −2.0	45,070
−2.0 to −1.5	103,350
All brighter than −1.5	214,370

Fig. 34. *Above:* Boyden Observatory on Harvard Kopje near Bloemfontein, Orange Free State, South Africa, where several photographic telescopes observe the southern stars and galaxies. *Below:* Another view showing the 60-inch Rockefeller reflector.

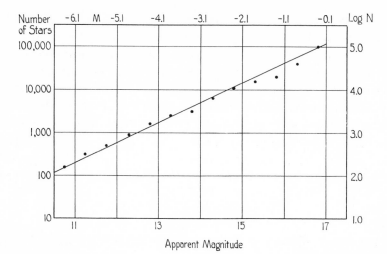

Fig. 35. The preliminary general luminosity curve for the brightest stars in the Large Cloud. Each point represents the total number of stars in the whole Cloud brighter than the corresponding magnitude. The vertical number scale is logarithmic. The straight line indicates, for example, that there are 10,000 stars brighter than photographic magnitude 14.6, which corresponds to absolute magnitude −4, approximately.

great richness of this neighboring galaxy. Absolute magnitude −6.5 corresponds to apparent magnitude 12.1 in the Large Cloud and to a luminosity about 60,000 times that of the sun; absolute magnitude −1.5 corresponds to about 600 times the solar brightness. The fainter we go, the more stars. If the number in each magnitude interval were to increase with decreasing luminosity in the same way as in the sun's neighborhood, the population of the Large Cloud would rise to more than 40,000 million stars! This is an appalling number, but it is probably but a fifth of the number of stars in our own larger and more luminous galactic system.

The actual rate of increase in number of stars with decreasing brightness is, however, unpredictable. Except for the giant and supergiant stars represented in Table 1, the general luminosity curves for the Magellanic Clouds are undetermined and essentially unattainable. Our failure to reach easily the main-line average stars is one price we must pay for the advantage of being ouside the Clouds.

Later it will appear that the Large Cloud is apparently a galaxy that is about average in dimensions and mass. But it does not follow that the luminosity curves, or the cepheid phenomena, are typical or average; they may be quite different for spheroidal galaxies and for the globular nuclei of spiral systems. Also the various characteristics of the star population vary from one part of a galaxy to another. Such heterogeneity prevails not only in distant spirals and in the Magellanic Clouds but also in our own Galaxy. The solar environment and the galactic nucleus are distinctly unlike. General luminosity curves (all star types together) for whole systems, therefore, do not amount to much in galactic interpretation, except perhaps for the spheroidal galaxies and globular clusters where supergiant stars are rare and a smooth uniformity appears to prevail.

Tools That Are Not Sharp Enough

The spread in the angular sizes of open clusters, mentioned in the preceding chapter, is excellently shown in the Large Cloud, and this diversity implies similar spread in linear sizes. Figure 36 illustrates the situation, which is indeed disappointing if we have hoped to find that the diameters are sufficiently alike to permit the distance of a cluster in our Milky Way to be judged accurately by the angle

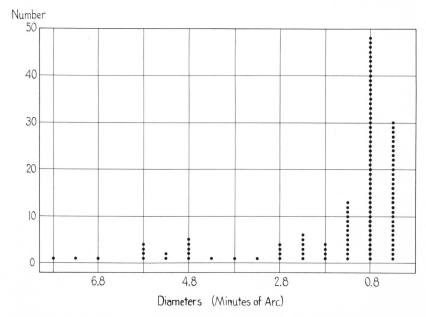

Fig. 36. Frequency of the angular diameters of the open clusters in the Large Cloud. One minute of arc corresponds, at the distance of the Cloud, to about 50 light-years.

it subtends. But the true spread in diameters is too much. In the Large Cloud, open-cluster diameters vary from 15 light-years and less to 300 light-years and more; the average of those measured is 40 light-years. If we assume that the *average* linear diameter applies to a given open cluster in the Milky Way, we may be off by 50 percent either way, and the error in diameter carries over directly as an equal error in the estimate of distance.

It still holds that the small open clusters in the Milky Way are on the average more distant than the angularly large ones; but that is as far as it is practical to go at present. In the Magellanic Clouds the small clusters and large clusters are, of course, effectively at the same distance. The largest ones may be called "constellations" (my term) or "expanding associations" (Ambartsumian's name for clusters of this sort in the Milky Way).

Figure 37 illustrates the apparent futility of trying to use the brightest stars in open clusters as criteria of distance, for here again we find a very wide spread, in this case in the topmost luminosities of cluster members. We could hope that the fifth star (in order of decreasing brightness) might be useful here as with globular clusters. Its absolute magnitude might have been a "constant of nature"—always the same, or nearly so. But such is not the case, even approximately. In many clusters, for instance, the fifth star (counting from

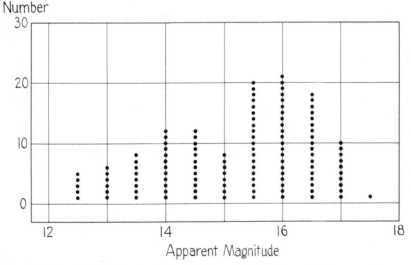

Fig. 37.   The wide distribution in the brightness of the fifth star in the open clusters of the Large Cloud. For half of the clusters the top stars are supergiants.

the very brightest) is 20,000 times as luminous as the sun, whereas for many other clusters the luminosity of the fifth star is only 500 times the solar luminosity.

Eventually our studies of the open clusters in the Magellanic Clouds should permit a new and definitive classification, and we may then transfer the results and techniques from the Clouds to our Galaxy and to others. Before that work is attempted, however, we should if possible have much additional information on star colors and star spectra in all of the suborganizations of the Magellanic Clouds. We may then find a practical way of using cautiously, for clusters of some of the subclasses, the diameters and magnitudes for estimating the distances of similar clusters in our own Galaxy.

In conclusion we note that the Clouds have been useful in showing that some tools are still too dull to be used effectively in the measurement of stellar distances and in the interpretation of galaxies.

4

The Milky Way
as a Galaxy

He who sees for the first time through a competent telescope the great star cluster in Hercules is definitely surprised, and naturally is skeptical when we offer the information, first, that each glittering point is a star far brighter than our sun, and second, that the whole concentrated globular assemblage of stars is so distant that the light now arriving has been en route for more than 300 centuries.

Star clusters of the globular form appeal to the imagination as well as the eye. They have enriched the general field of cosmography by contributing two important items to our knowledge of galaxies. They first indicated clearly that the sun and planets are eccentrically located in the Milky Way, far distant from the center in Sagittarius; and second, through their cepheids, they have helped to indicate the generality of the period-luminosity relation which first emerged as a tool for the measuring of sidereal distance in studies of another galaxy, the Small Magellanic Cloud.

Since the globular clusters have been useful in the portrayal of the Milky Way as a galaxy, we shall devote much of this chapter, which treats the Milky Way system as a cosmic unit, to discussions of clusters and of some strategically located variable stars.

Globular Clusters

The Hercules system has been so extensively studied during the past 50 years that we can now be sure of its great distance, its rich population, and the high luminosity of its brightest 10,000 stars. We know, for instance, that some of the stars are cepheid variables whose periods are correlated with absolute magnitude, and are therefore correlated with distance when apparent magnitudes are known. From the high background population of faint distant galaxies in the area around this cluster, we know that the intervening space must be quite transparent, and therefore that little or no correction to measures of magnitude and distance need be made on account of the absorption of light in space.

The Hercules cluster (Fig. 38) is commonly known by its number in the famous catalogue of nebulae and clusters of various kinds, compiled around 1780 by the French comet hunter, Charles Messier. The French astronomer needed for his comet-seeking a list of those unmoving sidereal objects that are not comets but look hazily like comets and therefore in small telescopes are misleading. (Many modern amateurs, and some professional astronomers as well, have come upon one of these Messier objects and without consulting catalogues have excitedly telegraphed the supposed discovery of a new comet to the information bureau at the Harvard Observatory.) Messier did not care much about clusters and nebulae as such, and he catalogued a hundred of them as nuisances. He is remembered for this catalogue; forgotten as the applause-seeking discoverer of comets.

The individual stars in Messier 13 (the Hercules Cluster) were, of course, not seen by Messier. "Nébuleuse sans étoiles," he records for the mighty Hercules swarm, and also for the 26 other globular clusters in his lists. It was left to the Herschels to resolve into stars

Fig. 38.   Number 13 in Messier's catalogue is the "Great Hercules Cluster," visible to the unaided eye. Its distance is about 30,000 light-years. (Harvard photograph, 16-inch telescope.)

most of the brighter globular clusters, and to the modern reflecting telescopes to resolve the faint ones.

The observers at the beginning of this century frequently suspected the existence of spiral arms and other structure in the brighter globular clusters, but these imagined structural details faded out of fact and memory with the increasing information given by the large reflectors, which show not hundreds of stars but tens of thousands. For a few clusters, wisps of dark nebulosity give a semblance of irregular form.

Practically all of the approximately 100 known globular clusters of our galactic system (Dr. Helen Hogg tabulated 106 in 1955) are smooth and smoothly concentrated to their centers, where the star density becomes too great for separating the individual stars, visually or photographically, as shown, for example, in Fig. 39. Short exposures, however, like a 3-minute "snapshot" (Fig. 40) of the Omega Centauri cluster of the southern sky, show the brighter central stars clearly; but when, with the same 60-inch reflector at

Fig. 39. NGC 2419, in the middle of the photograph, is a remote globular cluster. The cluster is the "intergalactic tramp" in Lynx, described on p. 81; it is probably more than 200,000 light-years away. (Palomar photograph, 200-inch telescope.)

the Boyden Observatory at Bloemfontein, we go down to the twentieth magnitude (Fig. 41), seeking stars as faint, intrinsically, as our sun, we "burn out" the center and stop practically all research on the cluster except at the outer edge.

A few globular clusters show in their projected images a slight elongation, indicating in some sectors an excess of stars of perhaps 10 to 15 percent. Omega Centauri is thus elongated, as can be seen by careful examination of the small-scale picture in Fig. 42. The deviation from circularity may indicate the existence of an equatorial bulge produced by rotation around a polar axis that is inclined at a considerable angle to the line of sight. Or it may register the result of past collisions and encounters, such as would be produced by the passage of the cluster through the star strata of our Milky Way. Or perhaps the cluster was born that way. We are still far from the full dynamical explanation of globular clusters.

Fig. 40.   Omega Centauri; a 3-minute exposure which permits the study of the central brighter stars. (Harvard photograph, ADH telescope.)

Fig. 41.   Omega Centauri; a 60-minute exposure which in reaching for the faint stars burns out the center. (Harvard photograph, ADH telescope.)

Fig. 42. Omega Centauri, to illustrate, on a small-scale photograph, the slight elongation that is also shown in Fig. 41. (Harvard photograph, patrol camera.)

Messier 13 is popular because its nearness and position in the sky make it available to more than 90 percent of astronomical observers. It can be seen with the unaided eye; and locating it (with the aid of a star map) is one of the interesting exercises for the beginner. Its identification should be in his permanent repertory, along with that of the Andromeda Nebula (Messier 31, Fig. 43), which is the only external galaxy readily visible to northern observers; neither of them is easily discerned, however, except on nonhazy moonless nights.

The amateur's list of naked-eye beacons in the sky should also include the Orion Nebula (Fig. 2), which is a true nebulosity about 1500 light-years away; and h and χ Persei (Fig. 44), a double open cluster in the northern Milky Way. (The Pleiades and the Hyades are open clusters that are too easy.) These four objects are good representatives of four important categories—globular clusters, open

Fig. 43.   The Great Andromeda Nebula, Messier 31, and its two small companions.
(Palomar photograph, 48-inch telescope.)

Fig. 44.   The double cluster h and χ Persei—a pleasant test for the naked eye. (Harvard photograph, 16-inch telescope.)

clusters, gaseous nebulae, and spiral galaxies—all visible with the unaided eye, and unforgettable after being seen with strong field glasses or small telescopes.

The far-south observer can also see the Orion Nebula and he can use Omega Centauri and 47 Tucanae as outstanding naked-eye globular clusters, the Magellanic Clouds as external galaxies, and Messier 11, or Kappa Crucis (Fig. 45) at the edge of the Coal Sack, for his open cluster. He has available, in fact, much richer fields of stars, and much brighter nebulae and clusters, than we have in the north.

Among the interesting globular clusters are:

Messier 3, near the pole of the Galaxy in Canes Venatici, distinguished for its many and much-studied cepheid variable stars with periods less than a day (Fig. 26);

Fig. 45. The bright cluster Kappa Crucis, which appears, on small-scale photographs, to dangle into the Coal Sack from an arm of the Southern Cross. The scale of this reflector plate is too large to show either Cross or Sack. (Harvard photograph, Rockefeller telescope.)

Messier 22 in Sagittarius, bright and near, in direction not far from the galactic center, and situated in the midst of a great star cloud in the Milky Way;

Omega Centauri and 47 Tucanae, conspicuous because of nearness and intrinsic giantism;

Messier 4, in the Scorpion, inconspicuous because of heavy intervening space absorption, though possibly the nearest of all globular clusters;

Messier 62, apparently somewhat malformed;

NGC 2419 (Fig. 39) a globular system found by C. O. Lampland. The cluster has been studied by Walter Baade, who finds it so distant (more than 175,000 light-years) that it might be considered not a member of our galaxy but rather an "intergalactic tramp," or a free and independent citizen of the local group of galaxies. A considerable number of these very faint and remote star systems are now coming to light on photographs made with Schmidt cameras.

Nothwithstanding some important differences in stellar composition, the globular clusters are remarkably alike in general appearance. On the basis of their central condensations, however, I have classified them into 12 categories. The observed concentrations are to some extent merely a reflection of their distances and the telescopic power used, and not a key to their internal structure. A few clusters, devoid of the usual rich population of giant stars, are what we call "giant-poor"; their globularity and dense population are revealed only when long-exposure photographs bring out the fainter stars. Until then they seem to be merely loose clusters of small population.

Curiously enough, almost all of the now known globular clusters were discovered by Charles Messier and the Herschels (Fig. 46) more than 100 years ago—discovered with small telescopic power as nebulous objects, not recognized as star clusters. The modern large reflecting telescopes had to be used, however, to show that these hazy objects really are star clusters, rather than round nebulae or galaxies; and the reflectors have also been used indispensably to analyze the brighter clusters in detail. Observations of clusters that

Fig. 46. A somewhat strange Herschel telescope in a South African field near Cape Town.

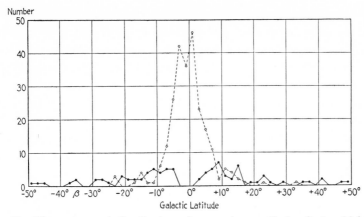

Fig. 47. The contrasted distribution of open clusters (*broken line*), which are crowded into the Milky Way band along the zero of latitude, and of globular clusters (*solid line*), which seem to avoid it. The few recent discoveries of globular clusters would not appreciably alter the graph.

are revolutionary for theories of stellar evolution have been made in recent years with the 200-inch Hale reflector on Mount Palomar by A. R. Sandage, H. C. Arp, W. A. Baum, and others.

Only a few new globular clusters have been picked up since 1900 in addition to the intergalactic tramps and those photographed in other galaxies. It appears that with the exception of those that lie behind dark obscuration, in the general direction of the galactic center, and except for some of the faint objects in high latitude (probably intergalactic), which are found on Schmidt camera plates, our Galaxy's family of about 100 globular clusters is already known. Photographs in red light will eventually disclose a few of the heavily obscured low-latitude clusters, and large-scale photographs may show that some of the rounded images along the borders of the Milky Way are in fact images of globular clusters rather than spheroidal galaxies, as now classified. S. van den Bergh speculates that one-third of all globular clusters are intergalactic. E. M. Burbidge and A. R. Sandage have analyzed two of the intergalactic systems and find them to be double the diameter of typical nearby globular clusters, but perhaps low in population.

Well before 1920 it was clear that the census of attainable globular clusters in our Galaxy was practically complete and therefore that the whole assemblage could profitably be studied as a system, as a unified aggregation of clusters. Peculiarities came to light at once when the newly estimated distances and the distribution on the sky were examined. It was found, in the first place, that the open Pleiades-like clusters of the Milky Way (galactic clusters, we sometimes call them) were closely concentrated to the galactic circle; they were immersed in rich star fields in all parts of the Milky Way band. Globular clusters, on the other hand, were found chiefly in the southern half of the sky and almost wholly outside the central belt of the Milky Way. This arrangement with respect to the Milky Way circle (the spread, that is, in galactic latitude) is shown in Fig. 47. The globular clusters are found in equal numbers on both sides of the galactic plane; they show a crowding toward the Milky Way, but suddenly disappear just short of its midmost zone.

Naturally the complementary distribution of globular and galactic clusters led to speculations on the possibility that the globular clusters are being absorbed by the Milky Way and there disintegrated and transformed into the poorer galactic clusters. But no clusters definitely in a transitional stage are found, and not more than two or three are suspects.

From the Heliocentric to the Galactocentric Hypothesis

We now know that the globular clusters are much more distant than most of the recorded galactic clusters, and that space absorption contributes strongly to the apparent absence of globular clusters from low galactic latitudes. Moreover, the globular clusters are not found in all galactic longitudes, as are galactic clusters; they are strongly concentrated in the constellations Scorpius, Ophiuchus, and Sagittarius (Fig. 48).

The center of the higher system of globular clusters was found, in my first analysis of the 93 objects then known, to be right on the Milky Way circle in the southern sky, close to the place where the three constellations come together. The right ascension is $17^h 30^m$, declination $-30°$, with the galactic longitude $325°$. The revised value of the present time differs but little: longitude $327°$, latitude $-1°$, with a probable error of half a degree. The corresponding right ascension is $17^h 40^m$, declination $-29°5$.

Rather early in the study of globular clusters a somewhat bold and premature assumption was made. Since the time when the idea was first proposed, however, no one has seriously objected, and

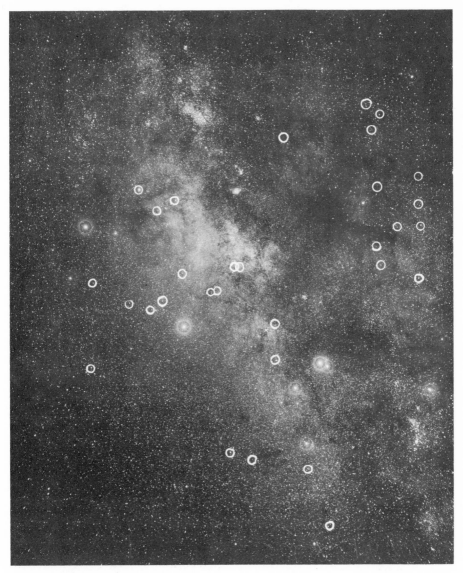

Fig. 48. Thitry-one globular clusters, almost one-third of all known in the galactic system, are shown on a single patrol-telescope photograph of the nucleus of our Galaxy. Circles enclose the cluster images.

many researches on stars, nebulae, and galaxies have tended to remove the assumption from the class of postulates to the class of accepted observations; we have, in fact, lost sight of the original presumption. It was proposed that the globular clusters represent, in a sense, the "bony frame" of the body of the galactic system. It was argued that the spatial arrangement of globular clusters shows the distribution of the billions of galactic stars—shows that the center of the Home Galaxy is in the direction of Sagittarius, for there lies the center of the super-system of globular clusters.

A new concept of the place of the observer in the stellar universe came as a consequence of these observations and arguments. The heliocentric theory was satisfactory for the planetary system, but no longer sufficient for the stellar system; the sun is no longer to be taken as central among the stars of the Galaxy, but rather as at some tens of thousands of light-years from the galactic nucleus. The fact that the globular clusters are found principally in the Southern Hemisphere comes from the circumstance that they are clustered around the nucleus of the discoidal Galaxy, not around the observer. And it follows that the reason the star clouds of the Milky Way appear somewhat brighter in the direction of Sagittarius and neighboring constellations than elsewhere is that the observer looks toward the rich central nucleus when he turns to galactic longitude 327°, galactic latitude −1°.

An easy picture of the form of the galaxy, and of our position in it, is obtained from the analogy with an ordinary thin watch. The observer on the earth is located very near the central plane, beneath the second hand; the galactic nucleus, in the Sagittarius direction, is at the center of the watch. We see the Milky Way band of stars when we look in any direction toward the rim of the watch, and more stars, of course (except when obscuring dust clouds intervene), in the direction of the center than elsewhere. When from our eccentric position we look out through the face or the back of the watch, we see relatively few stars; or, in other and more technical words, the star density decreases with increasing galactic latitude. It is, in fact, through the relation of star numbers to galactic latitude that we have deduced the watch-shaped contours of the galactic system.

A comparison with the edge-on spirals lends formidable support to the deduction that our Galaxy is discoidal in form. Around the central axis (of the minute and hour hands, in our analogy), the whole watch-shaped Galaxy rotates, but not as a solid (except near the central axis). The movement of most of the individual stars with respect to the center is probably along somewhat elliptical rather than exactly circular paths.

Details of rotation and internal structure, as far as we have now grasped them, are treated in *The Milky Way*. It is the responsibility of the present volume to look after the general aspects of the Galaxy as seen from outside. But first we should repeat that the hypothesis that globular clusters outline the Galaxy, and locate its center, has been supported thoroughly by work on stellar distribution, stellar dynamics, radio astronomy, and the motions and structural analogues in other spiral galaxies, for example, in NGC 891 (Fig. 49). The measures of radial and transverse motions of neighboring stars indicate that at our distance from the center (some 30,000 light-years), the speed in the orbit of revolution around the central axis is something like 140 miles per second, and the time required for one trip around—that is, the length of the "cosmic year"—is about 2 million terrestrial centuries. The foregoing numbers will be altered by further research, but they are certainly of the right order of magnitude.

The Thickness of the Galactic System

The analogy of the thin watch gives us the correct impression that the diameter of the Galaxy in its plane is five to ten times the thickness. But we must introduce two important modifications of the analogy. There can be little doubt that the central nucleus of our Galaxy is spheroidal, like that of many spirals (Fig. 9). We should therefore visualize a central bulge covering nearly a quarter of the face and back of the watch. But we do not find as sharp limits to the Galaxy as to the watch. The star population thins out with distance from the nucleus along the Milky Way plane, and also thins out with distance perpendicular to the plane. Analogously, the earth's atmosphere has no sharp boundaries but thins out with height indefinitely.

If we were a little more fully informed, we might say confidently that 99 percent of the stars of our Galaxy are within a watch-shaped, or discoidal, system of specific dimensions (it might be something like 100,000 light-years in diameter by 10,000 light-years in maximum thickness). Such statements can be accurately made about the mass of the earth's atmosphere—for example, 99 percent of it is below an altitude of 20 miles. But the best delimiting we can do at present with the Galaxy, working as we are from

Fig. 49. NGC 891, in Andromeda, showing its bulged-out central nucleus and the dust clouds along its equator. (Mount Wilson photograph, 60-inch telescope.)

a rather bad location inside, is to measure the most distant members possible in all directions and thus get at least mimimum dimensions. It is necessary, of course, to show that such distant stars are actually members, and not intergalactic. Eventually we may know enough about the laws of distribution of galactic stars to estimate accurately how much of the mass of the whole system lies within various given boundaries.

The total thickness of the Galaxy, with its centrally bulging nucleus, merits further study. In the all-inclusive system of globular clusters many are at large distances. Some are seen very far above the face of the "watch" and others far below its back. Except for a few very faint and distant clusters recently discovered on Schmidt camera plates, all clusters seem to be physical members of our Galaxy. We are led to wonder if isolated stars also extend out so far. If they do, the over-all shape of the whole Galaxy may not be like that of a watch; it may be spherical, or rather, it may consist of a central discoidal organization like a typical spiral galaxy, surrounded by a roughly globe-shaped "corona" or "haze" of outlying stars.

The existence of a surrounding haze of galactic stars was surmised many years ago, because faint cluster variables had been found in high latitudes—frequently near globular clusters, but apparently not members of them. The reality of this corona has now been definitely established through laborious and systematic studies of faint variables in many latitudes and longitudes. Thousands of stellar photographs, made with several telescopes located at the Cambridge, Bloemfontein, and Oak Ridge (Agassiz) stations of the Harvard Observatory, have been required for the discovery and measurement of the scattered variables. Comparable work has been done in Holland and Germany. The variables of the cluster type (the cepheids with periods less than a day) have been most useful; they have high luminosities (about 150 times that of the sun), and, of highest importance, they are found all over the sky. The long-period cepheids and the novae, both known as good indicators of distance, are not found in high latitudes and can assist but little in exploring the stellar haze. Moreover, the classical cepheids, as noted earlier, belong to two or more different populations and serve only when properly identified.

Variables fainter than the eighteenth magnitude can be found on some of the photographic plates used in the Harvard variable-star surveys. When such variables are proved to be cluster-type cepheids, for which the median absolute magnitudes are approximately zero, and when in the surrounding field many external galaxies are also photographed, indicating relatively little space absorption in that direction, then we can readily compute that the variables under study are approximately 40 kiloparsecs, or more than 125,000 light-years, distant. If, in addition, the variables are in the highest galactic latitudes, as far as possible from the Milky Way circle, then the measured distance from the earth is also the distance of the variables from the galactic plane. Thus we could find the half-thickness of the galactic system, the extent of the surrounding haze.

Actually we have not yet measured stars that distant in high galactic latitudes, but cluster-type variables between 30,000 and 50,000 light-years from the plane have been found on both sides. Moreover, these variables show so definitely a higher frequency as we approach the plane that we can with some confidence conclude that they are all, or nearly all, an organic part of the Galaxy (not intergalactic). It appears, therefore, that the surrounding haze of stars has a total thickness across the galactic plane that approaches, or perhaps exceeds, 100,000 light-years.

The best current value for the diameter of the Milky Way discoid in its own plane is also about 100,000 light-years, a quantity difficult to be precise about because of our awkward inside location and our troubles with the irregular clouds of absorbing dust and gas in low latitudes. Is there, perhaps, a star haze beyond the rim, as well as in high latitude—a haze that increases the over-all dimensions of the Milky Way system in the galactic plane? Have the faint cluster-type variables shown definitely, as suggested above, that the galactic system, because of its haze of stars, is essentially spherical in shape, with a heavy central discoidal structure that contains 99 percent of the stellar mass? Or does this haze of stars so extend in all latitudes that it gives to the surrounding sparsely populated haze the shape of a somewhat flattened spheroid, perhaps twice as extended in the Milky Way plane as at right angles thereto? Observations may eventually demonstrate this last and most likely hypothesis.

Measuring the Boundaries

The determination of the size of the neighboring large spiral in Andromeda can be made without much difficulty by making special long-exposure photographs and measuring them with densitometers. There is some difficulty, however, arising from the intervening stars of our own system, which are especially annoying when we attempt to measure the exceedingly faint star haze that extends far beyond the visible or ordinarily photographed bounds of the Andromeda system. Nevertheless, the measurement of this corona has been made, photographically and photoelectrically, as well as by the radio telescope. We shall record in the next chapter that the Andromeda system is found to be astonishingly large, in area and in volume, when all the outlying regions revealed by the densitometer tracings are included.

The measurement of the boundaries of our own system, as indicated above, is not so simple. The attack on the problem at the Harvard Observatory has produced, however, preliminary values of the extent of the main discoidal system. Since we are apparently well out toward the rim of the Galaxy, we take advantage of nearness to the boundary in the direction of the constellations Auriga, Taurus, and Gemini to explore that part of the Milky Way and look farther, if possible, into the surrounding haze and the space that lies beyond.

The study of our Galaxy's boundaries, when it involves the use of the numbers, sizes, and brightness of external galaxies, must be restricted to the higher latitudes, because the clouds of obscuration fairly well hide from us whatever galaxies there may be in a direction close to the Milky Way circle. In the anticenter direction there is of course heavy space absorption. We have not escaped the darkness by turning away from Sagittarius. We suspect sometimes that there may be around our Galaxy a continuous peripheral ring of obscuration, such as appears to be present in many external galaxies (Fig. 50). There are, however, in the anticenter region, some half-open windows in the obscuration, rather close to the Milky Way circle. Through the thinner dusty haze of these windows many far-distant galaxies can be dimly glimpsed. It is in such semi-transparent regions that the study of boundaries can best proceed.

Fig. 50. NGC 4594, with its strong peripheral band of obscuration. (Palomar photograph, 200-inch telescope.)

The program for the anticenter area was simply planned, but has been tedious in execution. All the sky on both sides of the Milky Way, within about 40° of the anticenter, has been profusely photographed with Agassiz Station instruments that can show variables to the seventeenth or eighteenth magnitude. Some assistance in the program has been given with the Cambridge and Bloemfontein telescopes. For each of the 160 separate fields a considerable number of photographs, made on different nights throughout a season, have been intercompared minutely, and changes in the image size of any of the several million stars photographed have been noted. These changing images indicate variable stars, most of them previously unknown. Measures of the photographed images on a large number of plates distinguish the various kinds of variables—eclipsing systems, long-period variables, irregular performers, and some cepheids. It is these cepheids that we have chiefly sought, since their periods, once derived, indicate at least approximately their absolute magnitudes. There has been much preliminary work with the sequences of standard magnitudes in order to obtain dependable values for the apparent brightness of the newly found cepheids. Once we have both apparent and absolute magnitudes, the photometric distances are immediately derived (see Chapter 3).

The measures of the distance of variables in the anticenter region, are, however, of little value unless we know that the magnitudes have not been vitiated by space absorption of unknown amount. At this point, therefore, another phase of the research on the anticenter was undertaken. It was possible to judge how much absorption affects one of the variable-star fields by counting for that area the number of external galaxies shown on long-exposure photographs made with the large-field "galaxy hunters"—the Bruce refractor and its successor, the Armagh-Dunsink-Harvard reflector, at the southern Boyden station, and the Metcalf doublet (Fig. 51) and Jewett reflector at the northern. When to the seventeenth magnitude, for instance, we find as many as 12 galaxies per square degree, we assume either (1) that space is wholly transparent and our computed distances of variable stars in that field will be safe and true, or (2) that the inherent irregularity in the distribution of galaxies has manifested itself in the area we explore, and that in spite of some space absorption (which corrupts the measured distances of the cepheids) the galaxies appear numerous only because an accidentally richly populated metagalactic region coincides with our variable-star field. There is nothing much to be done with this unhappy situation, arising from nonuniformities in the distribution of galaxies, except to smooth out such irregularities, and lessen the consequent errors, by dealing with large areas—by working in many adjacent fields of variable stars and with tens of thousands of galaxies.

The exploration of anticenter boundaries and of the galactic haze by means of the combined investigations on variable stars and galaxies in Auriga, Taurus, and surrounding constellations is similar in technique to researches elsewhere along and outside the Milky Way. In particular, we continue to seek the extent of our system in the direction of the galactic poles, and attempt to find the contour of the mid-galactic bulge as it may be revealed through studies of galaxies and variables in fields that are only 20° to 40° from the direction to the galactic center.

In the fields that border the great spheroidal central nucleus of our Galaxy, the stars are, of course, very numerous, and the vari-

Fig. 51. The Metcalf 16-inch doublet at the Agassiz Station (with companions);
it photographed 100,000 faint galaxies not heretofore known.

ables unusually abundant. In the highest latitudes a dozen variable
stars per 80-square-degree field is the average population shown
with the Metcalf doublet, but on the fringes of the nucleus more
than 100 variables are commonly found on one plate; and in the
richest of the southern star clouds in Sagittarius, Scutum, Scorpio,

and Centaurus, such plates, if deeply exposed, can show 1000 variables. In these most populous regions, however, which are usually in very low latitudes, we cannot as yet satisfactorily use the material to determine distances, because the external galaxies are completely blacked out and the amount of space absorption between us and the variable stars cannot be accurately estimated. It is practically a two-way axiom: rich in variables, poor in galaxies; rich in galaxies, poor in variables.

More About the Nucleus

It has been assumed without much question (and backed by a good deal of evidence) that our galactic system is a monstrous spiral galaxy of an open type. (The subject has been discussed at length in *The Milky Way,* chapter 4.) We have shown earlier in this chapter that we are located out toward where the haze begins, or nearly that far from the center of the Galaxy. If photographs similar in power to those we make were made of our galactic system from a suitable location in the Andromeda Nebula, they would show that most of our Galaxy's bright spiral structure is nearer to the center than we are: in fact, it might require very sensitive equipment to record any radiations from our immediate stellar neighborhood. The Andromedan observer should, however, easily photograph a few of our neighboring star clouds, like those in Perseus and Cygnus. The Pleiades should be seen as a faint cluster.

Formerly it was thought possible that our Galaxy would finally be revealed not as a single and simple class *Sb* spiral, but as something more complicated. It might have entanglements, such as would result if a Magellanic-type galaxy (and there are four of that type not so very far away) were at present crossing our galactic plane, or were near it. To unravel such an interloper from our star fields would trouble us a good deal. But now we think it unlikely that our Milky Way system is a multiple—a confused complex like Stephan's quintet (Fig. 52). The radio telescopes have pretty well disposed of that hypothesis. At present it is popular, and perhaps wise, to work with the simplest assumptions and maintain that our Galaxy in most details closely resembles a typical *Sb* galaxy like the Andromeda Nebula, or perhaps an *Sbc*.

Much of the obscuring material that conceals the galactic nucleus

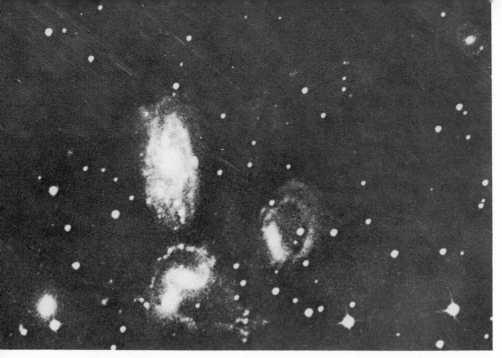

Fig. 52. The Stephan quintet of galaxies in Pegasus. (Mount Wilson photograph, 60-inch telescope.)

is at no great distance, only a few hundred or a thousand light-years away, and it probably has nothing to do with the nucleus itself. It is in part the dust that lies in the dark lanes between the spiral arms. But wherever the obscuring material may be located, it effectively conceals some of the nucleus, and probably dims it all to a measurable degree. Beyond the center there must be much dust, for in its general direction no external galaxies show through.

Hundreds of variable stars, and many star clusters and diffuse nebulae, have been studied in the Sagittarius area. Much remains to be done on the stars of the central mass (or galactic nucleus) that appears to be located 8 or 10 kiloparsecs (say 30,000 light-years) distant. It controls the motion of the sun and neighboring stars, and thus determines the length of the cosmic year.

In addition to results accuring from the direct assault on the problems of the galactic center by using photographs in blue, yellow, and red light, and by radio searches that penetrate the dust clouds, some advance can be made by exploring the fringes of the central ball where it extends 15° to 20° from the galactic circle and is moderately free of interfering dust. Also further useful investigation can be made along the Milky Way circle, north and south of the nucleus. In fact, the whole quadrant of the sky along the galactic circle from Centaurus through Sagittarius to Scutum demands

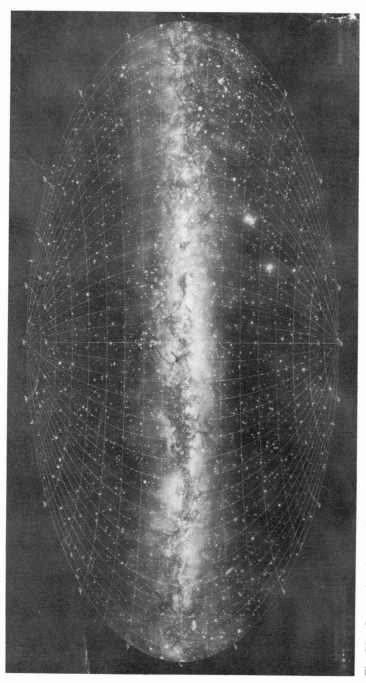

Fig. 53.   Composite picture of the Milky Way. (Lund Observatory.)

detailed exploration. This section appears as the central quarter of Fig. 53, a composite picture of the Milky Way. It shows on a small scale the sum total of light contributed by some thousands of millions of stars. It also indicates how heavily the dark lanes cut into the bright star fields, and how seriously we are handicapped in our researches by the chaotic clouds of obscuring material that shield from our curiosity some of the secrets of the galactic nucleus.

5

The Neighboring Galaxies

Neighborhood is a relative term, and indefinite. It depends on the speed of normal travel and communication, and on the size of the total domain. It implies a large non-neighborhood. The earth's persisting neighbor is the moon; comets are only occasional visitors. The neighbors of the sun can be taken as the stars within 50 or 100 light-years, with the billions in the Milky Way excluded. The planets and comets are not the sun's neighbors; they are just constituents of the sun's personal family.

The neighborhood of the Galaxy might be so defined that it includes only the Magellanic Clouds and some vagrant star clusters, all within a radius of 200,000 light-years; or enlarged so that its radius extends to 2 million light-years or so, and then the neighbors would be all the now-recognized members of the local group of galaxies. For the present chapter we choose to take as neighborhood this larger volume. But such a sphere is still relatively very small and leaves out of consideration practically all of the known and explorable universe—leaves out 99.99 per cent of it; nevertheless it does encompass about 10^{58} cubic miles.

The Triple in Andromeda, and Messier 33

The neighborliness of the Magellanic Clouds, and their useful cooperation in the task of exploring galaxies, has been recorded in two of the preceding chapters. The Andromeda group of galaxies, we find, is not as conveniently located when we want to borrow astronomical tools and obtain general cosmic information. The nearly 15 times greater distance of those neighbors conceals from us some of their inner secrets that would be useful if revealed, and perhaps would be easy to learn if they, too, were but 160,000 light-years away. Nevertheless, this neighborly group should be credited with leading us directly to basic knowledge of the outlying Metagalaxy.

Stated otherwise, the archipelago in Andromeda (and I like to associate with it the spiral Messier 33 in the adjacent little constellation of the Triangle, but not Messier 101, shown in Fig. 54, or Messier 81, Fig. 55) has provided preliminary steppingstones for our plunge into the metagalactic oceans of space and time, where with some success we now grasp at thousands of other "island universes," and glimpse a billion more on the cosmic horizons.

Each one of these four neighbors has contributed, but unequally, to our knowledge and our exploratory equipment. A preliminary report follows.

Messier 31 (Fig. 43), the "Great Nebula" in Andromeda, is a galaxy that has contributed more facts about the universe than any other spiral, thanks to its relative nearness, its novae, cepheids, supernova of 1885, globular star clusters, dust clouds, nebulae, high radial speed, and spectroscopically determined rotation. It provides the only opportunity that most Northern Hemisphere observers will ever have of seeing with the naked eye an external galaxy, of looking at a celestial object at a distance of more than

Fig. 54. Messier 101, although a neighbor, is not near enough to be a member of the local group. Its spectacular arms are recorded in another way in Fig. 70. (McDonald photograph, 82-inch telescope.)

10 million trillion miles without telescopic aid, and absorbing, in the process of looking, live bits of radiation that are some 400 times as old as the Pyramids of Egypt.

Messier 32, the slightly fainter of the two companions, has in-

Fig. 55. Another bright and beautiful neighboring galaxy, Messier 81, more than 3 million light-years distant and not within the local family. It has a small family of its own, as has Messier 101. (Palomar photograph, 200-inch telescope.)

formed us directly, through the researches of Sinclair Smith, that a typical spheroidal galaxy can be essentially barren of supergiant stars. Walter Baade has photographed its individual giant stars with the Mount Wilson 100-inch reflector, and has also resolved into stars the more elliptical companion, NGC 205, as well as the nucleus of Messier 31.

The two companions, through being about five magnitudes fainter than the Andromeda Nebula, illustrate the wide dispersion of galaxies in size and brightness. These small ellipsoidal galaxies serve as a link, so far as mass and luminosity are concerned, between average galaxies and the most gigantic of globular clusters. But in diameter they far exceed the average globular cluster.

Messier 33, like Messier 31, has yielded, chiefly through the spectroscopic studies by Mount Wilson and Lick Observatory workers, a richness of information useful in interpreting galaxies in general, especially with regard to internal motions and the maximum attainable brightness of variable and nonvariable supergiant stars.

The Andromeda Nebula, now to be treated in greater detail, is in right ascension $0^h 40^m$, declination $+40°$. It is rather easily picked up without telescopic aid on clear moonless autumn nights and winter evenings. Its class is *Sb,* closely resembling our Galaxy, which may, however, be a little more open, like *Sbc* or *Sc.* It lies 21° from the Milky Way circle, in a fairly rich field of foreground stars and background faint galaxies (Fig. 56a). The stars in the area are members of our Galaxy, at no great distance from the sun; all the nebulous objects, except some faint globular clusters that belong to the Andromeda Nebula, are external galaxies, which are probably without exception more than 10 million light-years distant. The richness of the field in stars, and especially in faint external galaxies, suggests that there is no heavy space absorption (light diminution) between us and the Andromeda triple.

Distances and Dimensions

How far away are Messier 31 and Messier 33—these nearest and most studied of spirals? The uncertainty of the answer is one of the grim prices we pay for being located in an irregularly dusty galaxy. We suffer uncertainty also from the weakness of our magnitude

Fig. 56*a*. A patrol-camera photograph showing Messier 31 and Messier 33, the two nearest spirals. Messier 31 is above the center, to the right; Messier 33, below and to the left, with the second-magnitude star Mirach just halfway between, in the middle of the photograph. The bright star to the far right and below the middle is the highly photogenic Sirrah (α Andromedae), which is also of the second magnitude. (Oak Ridge photograph by Henry A. Sawyer.)

scales fainter than the fifteenth magnitude. Moreover we have not yet a final decision on the zero point of our present period-luminosity relation. Certainly the Andromeda group is not as near as it appeared to be before the revised period-luminosity curve was deduced.

If we assume that the globular clusters of Messier 31 are closely comparable with those of the Milky Way system, then the distance is about 2 million light-years. If we depend on the cepheid variables (Fig. 57), and on recent revisions of the magnitude scale, we may put the distance at 2.5 million light-years. In any case we

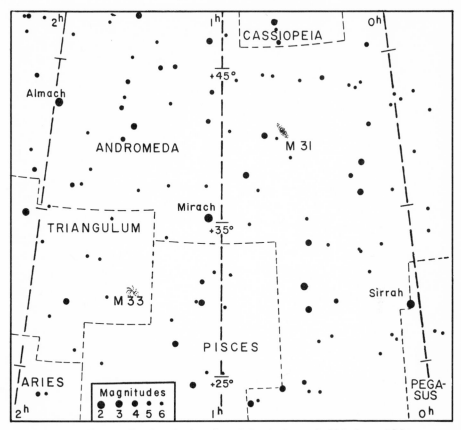

Fig. 56*b*.   A diagram showing the location of the Andromeda Nebula and Messier 33 among the naked-eye northern stars.

must allow for the effect of cosmic dust in our Galaxy and in the Andromeda Nebula itself. Better accord will doubtless be reached in a few years. Further work on colors, magnitudes, and spectra will clarify the characteristics of this giant neighbor of ours. From prolonged studies of the supergiant variable stars, Dr. Baade and Miss Henrietta Swope have derived valuable information about the inner structure. Incidentally, the dimensions of our own Galaxy may be somewhat revised after more attention has been paid to the colors of galactic cepheids and to the better fixing of the zero point of the period-luminosity curve.

For the further computations in this chapter we shall take 2 million light-years as the distance separating the centers of our

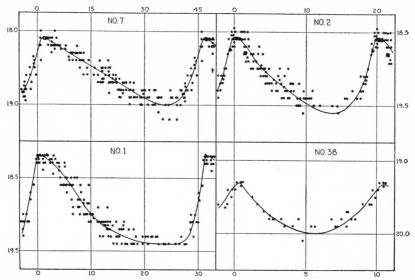

Fig. 57.   Light curves of cepheid variables in the Andromeda Nebula, as derived by Hubble at Mount Wilson.

Galaxy and Messier 31. The 175 miles per second recorded by the spectrographs as the speed of approach of Messier 31 is chiefly a result of our rotation around the axis of our system; we are approaching Messier 31, but the centers of the two galaxies are nearly stationary with respect to each other.

A further reference to the dimming of galaxies by interstellar dust will indicate why we may never get precise distances in metagalactic space. The order of the distances we shall get, but not values with negligible errors.

The long-exposure photographs show a great richness in background galaxies around Messier 33 and, as noted above, a fairly rich field around the Andromeda triplet. Hence a very moderate amount of absorption is tentatively adopted. Yet we cannot be sure of our procedure, for it may be that behind these neighboring spirals there chances to be not an average population but an excessive abundance of remote galaxies—an abundance that has been reduced, by means of a large amount of space absorption, toward the average for clear space.

Similarly, there might be a real metagalactic poverty, not richness, of galaxies behind the Small Cloud of Magellan where the nebular counts are low. But we assumed earlier that the low counts mean fairly heavy localized absorption, perhaps a "flare" of dust from the Milky Way, similar to the Cepheus flare that dims the North Polar region.

The hypothesis that great richness may in part balance absorption in the fields of Messier 31 and 33 is not so artificial as it may appear. In the next chapter we shall see that great inequalities in nebular distribution certainly exist. There are several extensive metagalactic clouds of galaxies, and one of them may lie in the direction of Andromeda and Triangulum.

We must, therefore, accept the unpleasant fact that the nonuniformity in space absorption and in the distribution of galaxies in metagalactic space leaves us unable to procure an exact measure of the distance to the nearest external galaxies, no matter how precise we eventually make our photometry of variable stars and novae, and no matter how securely we fix such factors as the zero point of the period-luminosity curve, the velocity of light, and the standards of apparent photographic magnitude.

We should mention one hope, however, and also one questionable benefit. The hope is that eventually, through refined measures of the colors of stars, we may correctly evaluate the dimming by dust, or side-step it. The dubious benefit of our inexactitude is that, because of this presently insurmountable difficulty with nonuniformity in the distribution of galaxies, as well as the uneven density of interstellar dust and gas, we need not labor now to reduce errors of observation to a difficult minimum in measuring metagalactic space. Rather rough values are the best we can hope for.

Messier 33, the open-armed bright *Sc* spiral of the Andromeda group, is 14° from Messier 31 The magnitudes of its cepheids indicate that it is at about the same distance from us as the Andromeda group. Accepting for the time being a distance from our Galaxy of 2 million light-years, we find that the separation of the two spirals is about half a million light-years.

How large are these nearest galaxies? The answer can be given precisely in linear units only when we have acceptable values for the distances; meanwhile, we give the angular dimensions. The main body of the Andromeda Nebula—the part of the system that is clearly shown on the best photographs with the best telescopes— is about 40 minutes of arc wide and 160 minutes of arc long. The surface area is seven times that subtended by the sun or moon. Taking the distance as 2 million light-years, the length of the main body of the Andromeda Nebula is about 92,000 light-years and the width, 23,000 light-years. It is reasonable to assume that the great spiral is actually circular in its equatorial plane, and that the elliptical form we observe is the result of foreshortening through tilt. The ratio of the length to the breadth, roughly 160:40, is therefore the measure of the tilt of its equatorial plane with respect to the line of sight. Since the tilt is only 15°, the object is viewed nearly edge on. The tilt of our galactic discoid as seen by an Andromedan observer is somewhat more, 21°—the galactic latitude of Messier 31.

To the unaided eye, or even to the eye assisted with a telescope, the Andromeda Nebula shows no spiral arms, and is much smaller than is shown by photographs such as that reproduced in Fig. 43. It appears scarcely larger than a bright star seen through haze. On the other hand, to the microdensitometer—that sensitive electrical apparatus now much used in measuring stellar photographs—it is much larger in length and width than shown by the best photograph, provided the plates for densitometric analysis are suitably exposed in properly chosen telescopic cameras. Densitometer tracings have indicated, as mentioned in the preceding chapter, that the boundaries lie far from the nucleus. Several astronomers have measured this corona or haze of stars that surrounds the main body of the system. My early measures of the angular dimensions increased the length of the photographic image from 160 minutes of arc to 270 minutes of arc, and the width from 40 to 240 (see Fig. 58). My values, however, were not verified by other investigators. In particular, the measure of the minor axis was called in question: it would indicate the existence of a thin spheroidal corona of faint stars like that now generally accepted for our own Galaxy.

But the major-axis increase of 70 percent, shown by my densitometer measures has been amply confirmed through the finding by the California observers of nebulosity and blue-white supergiant stars far out along the major axis, some of them 150 minutes of arc from the center. Recently (1959) the radio astronomers at Jodrell Bank, Manchester, England, have found that the minor axis of the radio corona, when measured at 408 megacycles per second with high-resolution equipment, is 360 minutes of arc

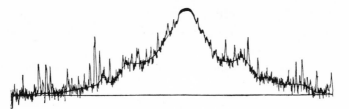

Fig. 58. Densitometer tracing along the major axis of Messier 31. Field stars and
plate graininess contribute to the irregularities; the undifferentiated starlight within
Messier 31 provides the larger trends in the tracing.

(200,000 light-years), and the major axis, 600 minutes of arc
(more than 300,000 light-years!). The radio measures therefore
given an over-all size of nearly 50 square degrees—considerably
larger than the Bowl of the Big Dipper. It is not certain that my
optical tracings and the radio measures refer to the same radiators,
but the evidence appears good that Messier 31 and our Galaxy are
discoids surrounded by a vast thinly populated corona.

The masses, population, and total luminosities of nearby galaxies
can now be roughly estimated but not precisely measured. An
obstacle to success in these ventures lies in the necessity that we
must compute and analyze on the basis of uncertain assumptions.
We could probably all agree that the mass of Messier 31 is not less
than the mass of a billion suns, nor more than the mass of a trillion.
In fact, we might boldly go further and put the lower and upper
limits of the mass, and the number of standard stars, at 100 billion
and 400 billion.

One way of estimating the mass more closely involves the use of
the total intrinsic luminosity (candlepower) of the galaxy, that is,
its absolute magnitude M, which is known just as accurately as we
know the distance d and apparent magnitude m, since by definition
it is $M = m + 5 - 5 \log d$. If the Andromeda Nebula were populated only by ordinary G stars, like the sun, we would compute
easily both its population (16,000,000,000 stars) and its mass
(16,000,000,000 solar masses), from the value for its total luminosity, which we take as absolute magnitude -20.0, 25.5 magnitudes
brighter than the sun. Or we could derive a good estimate of the
total mass if it were correct to assume that, although the stars in
the Andromeda Nebula are not all like the sun, the ratio of mass
to output of light for all of them is the same, on the average, as we
find for the sun—in other words, if the ratio mass/light = 1.0 in

terms of the sun as unit of mass and unit of light. Or we could succeed even if there were a different ratio, provided we knew what that ratio is.

Many of the stars that constitute the Andromeda Nebula are giants and supergiants, with more light emission per unit of mass than prevails with stars like the sun; for them the ratio mass/light is less than average; but certainly most of the stars are fainter and denser than the sun, of lower radiating efficiency, yielding much less light per unit of mass. For these dwarfish stars the ratio mass/light is much greater than 1.0. We have little information for any galaxy, including our own, on the relative numbers of supergiants, giants, average stars, dwarfs, subdwarfs, and dust particles. We might assume for computational purposes that the average mass/light ratio elsewhere is about like that pertaining to the solar neighborhood, where there are many dwarfs and few giants. Ernst Öpik made this assumption years ago and derived for Messier 31 the value mass/light = 2.6, and a total mass of 4.5 billion solar masses. With a more modern value of the absolute magnitude, his value for the total mass would have been much larger, possibly 25 billion solar masses.

The mass/light ratio varies greatly, no doubt, throughout the diverse structures of our own galactic system, and also in the Magellanic Clouds, in the Andromeda Nebula, and everywhere. We may find the ratio to be 100 or more in the outer parts of the great spirals, where there appears to be much mass and little light. This luminosity method of getting at masses and populations is obviously not very useful.

A second method, which would be better if we knew how to use it wisely, involves the measure of mass through observations of motions inside the galaxy, as revealed by the shifts of the spectral lines. The work at the Lick Observatory on Messier 31 by Babcock, and on Messier 33 by Mayall and Aller, was important and difficult but we do not yet know for either spiral just how the stars and masses are distributed in the regions where the line shifts and motions were measured. Consequently we cannot definitely interpret the motions in terms of mass. As it stands the method implies, according to Mayall and Wyse, a total mass of about 100 billion suns for Messier 31 and less than 2 billion for Messier 33.

The gravitational control of the stars in a spiral differs from that in our solar system, where essentially all the mass is concentrated in the central sun and the controlling force varies inversely with the square of the distance from the center; and it differs also from what would prevail if the spiral were a discoidal body rotating as a solid with the force varying directly with the distance from the center. The actual situation probably lies between these extremes; and the composite law governing the motions of the stars in a galaxy certainly changes with distance from both the nucleus and the spiral arms. The accurate solution of the mass and population problem by way of spectrum-line shifts for individual stars within a spiral will therefore be difficult, but not necessarily hopeless. At best, however, we can explore observationally only the nearest and brightest galaxies for many years to come. Let us hope that these nearest reachable neighbors are sufficiently typical to lead toward knowledge of universal behavior.

A third, and so far the best, method of mass estimation involves the derivation of the relative motions in double-galaxy systems. As in the solar system, the orbital motions are a measure of the masses. Erik Holmberg and Thorton Page have specialized in this inquiry and have made ingenious use of the accumulating data on pairs of galaxies. From a discussion of 65 pairs, Page derives a preliminary value for the mass of an average galaxy of 250 billion suns, and an average value for the ratio mass/light of 18 in solar units. A highly significant result is that the giant spheroidal galaxies are on the average about 13 times as massive as the typical spirals and irregulars—400 and 30 billion suns, respectively. The mass/light ratio is only 1.3 for the irregulars and 41 for the spheroidals. These numbers apply, of course, only to the sample available, which preferentially includes giants; when velocities for fainter galaxy pairs are measured, the differences between spiral and spheroidal systems will probably be much reduced.

There is a somewhat vaguer method of finding the masses of external galaxies than those we have just mentioned, namely, the deduction of what the mass of a large cosmic unit ought to be from considerations of the basic nature of matter, time, and space. But the observed spread in size and mass, as illustrated by the giant Andromeda Nebula and its two small companions, disqualifies before we start the application of such a method to an individual galaxy. It has been seriously considered by only a few workers in cosmogonic theory.

And finally, there is a possibility of extending the double-galaxy technique of mass determination by calculating average masses from observations of motions of individual galaxies in the clusters and clouds of galaxies. This method will be based on the observed interactions between neighboring systems, and on theory. Again we shall need to assume that we know correctly the relevant laws of motion. Preliminary results have been obtained for the Virgo Cloud, but it may be that the simple assumptions concerning forces, which are good for planets, comets, and double stars, will betray us when we employ them on the macrocosmic scale appropriate for clusters of galaxies moving in clouds of intergalactic dust and neutral hydrogen gas.

As comment on the dimensions and populations of the other three objects in the Andromeda-Triangulum group of neighboring galaxies, a few sentences should suffice. Since the distances of Messier 33 and of the two companions, Messier 32 and NGC 205, are about the same as for Messier 31, we can use for them the same relation between the angular and linear dimensions, that is, the same relation between the minute of arc and the light-year: $1' = 600$ lt-yr. Dimensions and luminosities are given in Table 2. The average spiral of our catalogues is a little smaller and fainter than Messier 33; its luminosity is about 500 million suns.

For Messier 33, two sets of values are tabulated; the first is based on microdensitometer tracings from a long-exposure plate made with a 4-inch camera at the Agassiz station of the Harvard Observatory; the second set of values refers to the main body of the spiral as shown by a good photograph with a large reflector, such as the picture reproduced as a negative in Fig. 82. The measurable dimensions,

TABLE 2. *Dimensions and luminosities of four neighboring galaxies.*

Galaxy	Dimensions		Luminosity (10^6 suns)	Galaxy class
	Angular (min of arc)	Linear (light-years)		
M 31	160 × 40	92,000 × 23,000	10,000	*Sb*
M 33	90 × 60[a]	54,000 × 36,000[a]	600	*Sc*
	60 × 30[b]	36,000 × 18,000[b]		
M 32	8.5 × 7.5	5,000 × 4,500	120	*E2*
NGC 205	8 × 4	4,800 × 2,400	30	*E5*

[a] Microdensitometer value.
[b] Photographic estimate.

angular and linear, depend on photographic-exposure lengths, and the tabulated values are therefore too small if the spread of the scattered outlying stars is accepted as defining the size.

We estimate the tilt of Messier 33 as 30°, basing the result on direct measures of the best photographs. It is possible that the microdensitometer, which gives a much larger value for the minor diameter of the galaxy, is again, as for the Andromeda Nebula, measuring the sparsely populated enveloping haze of faint stars that surrounds the flattened spiral.

Stellar Types in Messier 31 and Messier 33

There is a concluding question to ask about this group of four neighbors: What kind of stars are they made of?

Cepheid variables are the most important from a general point of view because their magnitudes lead to knowledge of luminosities and distances, and their location in the spiral structure bears on the distribution of dark nebulosity. More than 40 cepheids are known in Messier 31 and the survey is not complete. Nearly as many are reported by Hubble in Messier 33. Also there are recognizable supergiant stars that are not variable. The individual stars in Messier 32, NGC 205, and the nucleus of the Andromeda Nebula were first revealed in 1943 on Baade's reddish-light photographs with the Mount Wilson 100-inch reflector.

Most of the work on novae in nearby galaxies has been done with the Mount Wilson reflectors, first by Hubble, later by H. C. Arp. In Messier 31 more than 100 novae have been found and the census was far from complete even in the years when a regular search was maintained. Arp estimates that 26 novae occur there every year. We remember that Messier 31 is a spiral of the inter-mediate class *Sb*. In Messier 33, Class *Sc*, only a few novae have been recorded, notwithstanding careful watching; and in the more open-type galaxies—the Magellanic Clouds—novae appear to be remark-ably scarce.

Fifty Million Andromedan Novae on the Way

The behavior of such violently disturbed stars as the novae must be studied in many systems for many years before we can be sure of their contribution to our knowledge of stellar evolution. (A typical

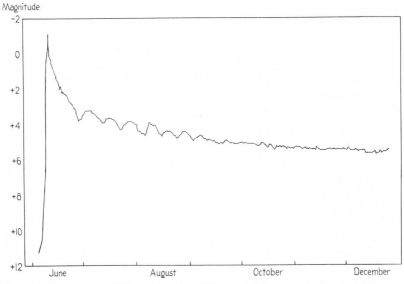

Fig. 59. Light curve of Nova Aquilae, 1918, the brightest nova discovered in our Galaxy since Kepler's supernova of 1604.

light curve is shown in Fig. 59.) Meanwhile it is interesting to record that if the present rate of "novation" holds for Messier 31—and we see no reason why it should not—there has been in the past 2 million years much as yet unrecorded stellar violence. The complete records of the light eruptions, confused radial motions, and spectrum changes for about 50 million novae are in the light waves on their way from the Andromeda Nebula to the earth—phenomena of the past for that evolving galaxy, of the future for us.

In addition to cepheids and novae, supergiant stars, as noted above, are clearly shown in the outer parts of both Messier 33 and Messier 31. Little is accurately known about them. They are too faint; and the background and foreground of fainter unresolved stars complicate the study of those that can be singled out. Moreover, the distance from the observer is so great that groups of stars like the Pleiades and some gaseous nebulae are merged into single tight images. Sometimes, because of this compactness the composite images are not recognized as representing clusters, or nebulae involving stars. They look like single supergiant stars. When used as though they were single stars, in estimating galaxy distances, they lead to erroneously small values. Because of this failure to recognize such compact clusters and compact bright nebulosities (H II regions), most of the distances of galaxies estimated by Hubble require revision upward.

A considerable number of large open clusters have been correctly recognized in Messier 31 and Messier 33, and many gaseous nebulae and star clouds as well. There are also many faint, fuzzy, circular images around the main body of Messier 31 that are now accepted as globular clusters, similar to the outlying globular clusters of our own galactic system. These clusters seemed at first to be somewhat smaller and fainter than the average globular cluster in our Galaxy, but with the revision of the cepheid zero point the discrepancy has been removed.

We shall eventually approach a fuller interpretation of these neighboring spirals by using the equipment in the astronomical tool house described in Chapter 3, that is, through more detailed studies of the somewhat analogous Magellanic Clouds, which are near enough for easy distinctions to be made between open and closed clusters, blue and yellow stars, diffuse and planetary nebulae.

The studies of the stellar contents of spirals have, nevertheless, proceeded far enough to assure us that our Galaxy, Messier 31, Messier 33, and other open spiral systems are of the same genus, and probably have not only the same population characteristics, but closely similar structures.

Two Other Irregular Neighbors

Up to this point we have accounted for seven members of the local group of galaxies. Our galactic system, the Magellanic Clouds, the Andromeda Nebula and its two companions, and Messier 33 have been sketchily described. Now we register two other members. One is Barnard's galaxy (Fig. 60), which carries the number 6822 in the New General Catalogue, and the other, found by Max Wolf of Heidelberg, is No. 1613 in the *Index Catalogue* that was compiled by J. L. E. Dreyer of the Armagh Observatory to help astronomers in the orderly study of newly discovered clusters and nebulae.

These new additions to our census of the galactic neighborhood are also irregular in form, like the Magellanic Clouds, and both are dwarfs. They may also be flattened, but the shapes of such systems in three dimensions are not easily proved. In actual luminosity, they are fainter even than NGC 205 and Messier 32. Their irregular

Fig. 60. Barnard's galaxy, NGC 6822, faintly shown through a southern star field. (Mount Wilson photograph by Hubble, 60-inch telescope.)

structure and low luminosities are very significant in our consideration of the make-up of the Metagalaxy. Four out of nine of the
nearby objects so far considered are misshapen and confused aggre-
gations of stars, whereas we find in our general surveys of the
Metagalaxy, for instance, down to apparent magnitude 12.8, that
only 3 or 4 percent of the galaxies are irregular in form. Of the
brightest thousand, about 75 percent are spirals, a little over 20
percent are spheroidal, and the remainder are irregular.

Why this difference for irregulars—45 percent to less than 5
percent? Is our part of the universe not typical of the whole? Or is
there something defective in our surveys? Or are the laws of chance
playing tricks?

The trouble is obviously with the surveys. The dwarfs are recorded
only if they are near; the giants are recorded over much greater
distances. Therefore the catalogue of the thousand brightest favors
the giants, and these giants in luminosity are preferentially spirals
and spheroidals.

Two of the nearby irregular objects are of very low total luminosity. If they were located 50 million light-years away, instead of less
than 1 million, our best photographs might not show them at all.
Also, if IC 1613 and the Small Magellanic Cloud were near the
faintest limit of the photographic plate, we might fail to see their
irregularity and would proceed to class them with the spheroidal
types; or we might mistake irregular extensions as spiral arms and
put them down as some kind of spiral galaxy.

NGC 6822. Dr. Edward E. Barnard was an inspired amateur living in Nashville, Tennessee, when, in 1884, his small telescope picked up, not far from the southern Milky Way star clouds, a faint nebulous patch, which was later labeled 6822 in Dreyer's catalogue. It is a difficult object and requires considerable telescopic power to show the mixture of stars and nebulosity (Fig. 60). The proper tool, of course, is the well-exposed photographic plate. Visual observations suffer from the complexities common to photometry of faint surfaces. Hubble has pointed out the interesting circumstance that with a low-power eyepiece on a 4-inch telescope the object is "fairly conspicuous—but barely discernible at the primary focus of the 100-inch." The former concentrates the light; the latter spreads it out.

Lying in the constellation Sagittarius (R. A. $19^h 42^m$; Dec. $-15°$), Barnard's galaxy is within the reach of the Mount Wilson reflectors and its distance, dimensions, and stellar content have been studied by Hubble. Eleven cepheid variables have been recognized and therefore the distance can be estimated. The Milky Way is only 20° away, and in consequence an unknown amount of light dimming by cosmic dust affects the photometric measures. NGC 6822 in many ways resembles the Magellanic Clouds. Its cepheids are typical. Figure 61 reproduces its period-luminosity relation. Again we note that the cepheid phenomenon is widespread among giant and supergiant stars.

The distance of Barnard's galaxy is approximately 1 million light-years—less than the distance to the Andromeda group, greater than the distance to the Magellanic Clouds. Its spectrum shows a small blue shift, indicating that relatively the observer and NGC 6822 are *approaching* each other; the speed is about 22 miles per second, according to Lick and Palomar measures. But this apparent approach comes from the observer's rotational speed in his own galaxy. The center of the Galaxy and NGC 6822 are *receding* from each other at the rate of 60 miles per second.

Unlike the Magellanic Clouds, this more distant dwarf galaxy is scarcely in the satellite class, for it lies far beyond the most remote cluster-type cepheid yet found in the Galaxy's surrounding star haze.

IC 1613. The dwarf irregular galaxy, IC 1613, in right ascension $1^h 0^m$, declination $+1°.6$, is far from the Milky Way plane, and measures of its distance and brightness are therefore little affected by obscuring dust (Fig. 62). Baade had this pygmy galaxy under

Magnitude

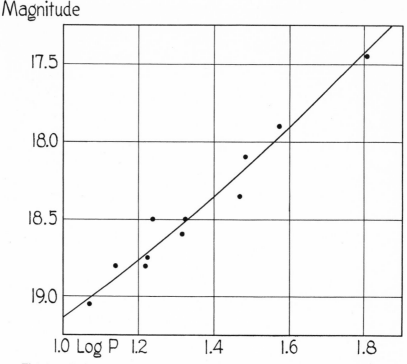

Fig. 61.   Period-luminosity relation for Barnard's galaxy. (After Hubble.)

careful observation at Mount Wilson for many years. From the many cepheid variables we can estimate 1,800,000 light-years as a provisional value of the distance. The total absolute magnitude of about −14.0 indicates that the luminosity of IC 1613 is the equivalent of only 60 million suns—a small affair compared with our own Galaxy, which is more than 150 times brighter. Still we call them both galaxies.

Unusual Neighbors in Sculptor and Fornax

Prior to 1938 the gamut of galaxy types had presumably already been run. All the forms had long been fully described. There were spirals, spheroidals, irregulars, with many variations on the spiral theme. Then in 1938 Harvard plates unexpectedly yielded two sidereal organizations of what appeared to be a new type.

Not much is yet known about these newly found neighbors in Sculptor and Fornax. I have written three short papers concerning

Fig. 62.   IC 1613, an irregular neighbor that is rich in cepheid variables. (Mount Wilson photograph, 100-inch telescope.)

them; Baade and Hubble have written one. A. D. Thackeray has used the Pretoria reflector to find in them hundreds of variable stars. Perhaps not a great deal needs to be known about them. They are relatively simple. And already they may have made their most significant contribution by revealing themselves as members of our local family of galaxies, and by possessing such low luminosities that they increase to six (out of eleven) the number of dwarfs in our neighborhood. This last implies that our earlier knowledge and assumptions concerning the average galaxy may need serious modification. Moreover, the estimates of the total number of external organizations and of the total mass of the Metagalaxy are involved. The finding of the Sculptor system is worth recounting in some detail.

The Sculptor Object. When the examination of plate 18,005 in the Bruce telescope series showed a couple of thousand faint and distant galaxies, in addition, of course, to about 30,000 intervening stars of our galactic system, we were not surprised. The plate was of good quality; the galactic latitude in Sculptor is high, far away from the Milky Way dust; the galaxy catch was about normal. But when it also showed in one region a uniform swarm of images at the limit of visibility, we could at first hardly believe that, in this clustering of spots on the big glass negative, the Metagalaxy was revealing something real and new. The swarm looked suspiciously like a darkroom unhappiness—fingerprints during development, perhaps —or a misadventure with the photographic film during manufacture.

The smooth undistinguished appearance of the Sculptor object on the photographic plate was much like the diagram in Fig. 63, for which the scale is the same as for the original photograph, but the number of spots in the figure should be everywhere multiplied by 2.5 to record correctly the number of objects shown by plate 18,005 in the square degree centered on the group; actually it spills over the bounds of this square degree. It is about 75 minutes of arc in diameter and contains 10,000 members brighter than magnitude 19.5.

The suspicion that the Sculptor object might be spurious disappeared at once when a confirming photograph was made. Also an old plate was found in the Harvard collection which as early as 1908 hazily recorded this interesting system. This early photograph was made, not with the Bruce refractor, the most powerful galaxy hunter at that time in the Southern Hemisphere, but with a tiny patrol camera that has a lens only 1 inch in diameter and a focal length of 13 inches. The plate was made by S. I. Bailey, while on a site-testing expedition to South Africa. His photograph had a total exposure of 23.3 hours. To obtain an exposure of that length, the best parts of the nights of October 9, 10, 12, 13, and 14 were used. His effort sufficed to record 80,000 galactic stars, and very

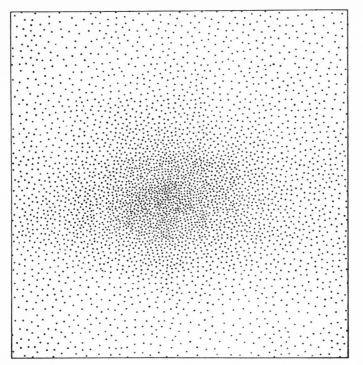

Fig. 63. A diagram illustrating the distribution of stars in the smooth Sculptor cluster. One square degree is represented.

dimly to register this unusual Sculptor object. If its position had not already been known when, seeking confirmation, we reexamined these old South African plates, the object would have escaped detection on them, or, if seen, would have been passed over as one of the occasional background variations on photographic film. The more modern and faster patrol cameras now at southern stations, show the object when the exposures are but 3 hours long; but even they show it only as a circular, slightly concentrated smudge. It requires large telescopes to resolve the system into its individual members.

Eventually Harvard's South African 60-inch reflector demonstrated that the members of the Sculptor object are stars, not faint external galaxies. We then had the problem of interpreting the system. If it had been a cloud of galaxies, of the sort we shall discuss in a later chapter, it would not have been very unusual, although its high population would have made it outstanding. As a cloud of stars it is not quite so easy. Scarcely a member is brighter than the eighteenth magnitude, and most of those on record are fainter than the nineteenth. Is the group inside our Galaxy or outside? Either the system must be very remote, with the brightest stars giants as usual, or it is inside our Galaxy and these top stars are dwarfs, appearing faint because they are really of low luminosity.

Fortunately the cepheids again come to our rescue. Two regular cepheid variable stars, first noted by the Mount Wilson observers, have been measured on the Harvard plates. The plate material is as yet scanty, but it indicates a distance of nearly 300,000 light-years.

The Sculptor object is in high latitude and we need make no substantial allowance for space absorption. In fact, the 2000 faint galaxies on the original Bruce plate confirm the assumed high transparency of intervening space. We can be pretty sure, moreover, that there is no serious obscuration within the system itself, because a number of external galaxies, tens of millions of light-years away, are visible right through the distended cluster of stars.

Knowing the distance, we calculate the diameter, and find that the Sculptor system has the dimensions of a galaxy, not the dimensions of an ordinary star cluster in the galactic system. And we conclude that this object, which is only twice as far away as the Magellanic Clouds and therefore is a member of our family of galaxies, is a dwarf in mass and luminosity.

Unlike IC 1613 and the Magellanic Clouds, which are irregular in form, the Sculptor galaxy is beautifully symmetric. The inner part, as Fig. 63 faintly indicates, is slightly elliptic; the outer bounds appear to be nearly circular. It has, in fact, the form of a globular star cluster, but the diameter of an average galaxy; and like the globular star clusters it is devoid of supergiant stars such as dominate both Clouds of Magellan and some of the other irregular galaxies. The Sculptor system also differs from the Magellanic type of galaxy in the absence of open clusters and bright gaseous nebulosities. It differs from a spiral galaxy in its obvious lack of structural detail, and from the typical spheroidal galaxy in its openness. The typical spheroidal galaxies are also free of supergiant stars. If one of them were brought to the distance of the Sculptor galaxy and nine out of every ten stars were removed, the remnant would probably resemble this new-type system in Sculptor.

The foregoing comparisons and suggestions can be summarized by saying that the Sculptor galaxy is a dwarfish type of stellar system, similar in various characteristics to globular clusters, open clusters, giant spheroidal galaxies, and Magellanic Clouds, but differing from them all. It is in fact just a loose, low-luminosity, spheroidal galaxy, and probably not at all rare in the Metagalaxy.

The Fornax Object. Soon after finding the Sculptor galaxy, we discovered on the Harvard plates a similar system in Fornax, and for a time it seemed possible that such objects, so late in being found, might be very numerous, not only in the local galactic family but throughout space. We systematically made suitable photographs with a special camera to test the frequency of the Sculptor type of stellar system. One hundred fifty small-scale plates, covering something more than 15,000 square degrees of the sky, in galactic latitudes higher than 20°, failed, however, to show other objects similar to these first two discoveries. More than a third of the sky was covered. Some new globular clusters and a few new galaxies of the Magellanic type were found, but no more of the faint symmetric dwarf galaxies. The possibility of finding such objects if they are several million light-years distant is remote, and therefore we may forever have a disturbing uncertainty about the frequency of galaxies of low luminosity. But in the Virgo Cloud, described in the next chapter, many dwarfs are tentatively identified as galaxies of the spheroidal type by Gibson Reaves at Lick and A. G. Wilson at Palomar; Paul Hodge at Harvard has found 16 dwarfs out of a total population of 39 in a loose cloud of galaxies (in Fornax), and of these 12 are spheroidal like the prototype dwarf in Sculptor.

An analysis by Baade of some of the nearby dwarf galaxies, for example, NGC 185 and NGC 147, and two faint spheroidal systems in Leo, as well as the companions of the Andromeda Nebula, indicates that the Sculptor type is not greatly different from other symmetric dwarfs.

A major contribution in this field is Thackeray's discovery of more than 200 faint cluster-type variable stars in the Sculptor galaxy, thus augmenting the 40 reported by Baade and Hubble. He estimates that the system actually contains as many as 700 of these short-period cepheid variables.

The spheroidal dwarf galaxy in Fornax is about twice as distant as the one in Sculptor. Some globular clusters are associated with it, and they have helped to indicate the distance. Table 3 contains

TABLE 3.   *Data on the Sculptor and Fornax galaxies.*

Quantity	Sculptor	Fornax
Right ascension (1900)	$0^h\ 55\overset{m}{.}4$	$2^h\ 35\overset{m}{.}6$
Declination (1900)	$-34°\ 14'$	$-34°\ 53'$
Galactic latitude	$-83°$	$-64°$
Total photographic magnitude	9.0:	9.0:
Magnitude of brightest stars	17.8	19.3
Mean angular diameter	75'	65'

numerical data about the two systems. Additional work with large reflectors before long should provide better values of the distances and dimensions than are now available.

It has been fortunate that several of the neighboring galaxies are in latitudes so distant from the Milky Way circle that we have little concern about interfering space absorption. It remains quite possible, however, that there are several other members of the local group that are concealed or partially concealed by the cosmic dust in low galactic latitudes. Hubble listed three spirals, NGC 6946, IC 10, and IC 342, as possible members. Another, noted by me, is NGC 2427 in Puppis. Baade suggested IC 5152, photographed by D. S. Evans at Pretoria. Except for this last, they are all near the Milky Way, dimmed by its interstellar dust—and there is nothing much we can do about it. That these objects are not very distant can be claimed for some on the basis of their low velocities—they do not seem to be receding rapidly, perhaps not at all—and for others on the basis of their large angular dimensions and reddish colors.

A later census of the Galaxy's neighbors will doubtless include additional dim irregular dwarfs, similar to IC 1613. Several such candidates for admission to the local group are already on the plates made at Oak Ridge, Bloemfontein, Mount Hamilton, and Palomar.

Again it is well to remember, however, that possibly more than half of those we assign to the local family are in fact simply nearby members of the general metagalactic field, and that only our Galaxy, Messier 31, 32, 33, NGC 205, and the Megellanic Clouds are real members of a local gravitational association—one that resembles hundreds of the remote small groupings seen on existing photographs.

6

The Metagalaxy

"Thickly populated district" would be an appropriate sign to warn metagalactic travelers in the neighborhood of our Galaxy. Within a distance of about 2 million light-years we have already found a score of others. Two of them appear to be a match for the biggest galaxies known anywhere in the whole metagalactic world, but mostly they are dwarfs. Once we have emerged from the region of our local group of galaxies, the population appears to thin out remarkably. If we extend the survey to 6 million light-years, increasing the volume surveyed by 27 times, we add only another dozen objects. Future careful searching will probably double that number because it will bring to light many dwarf galaxies, such as those that help make populous the local neighborhood. But we feel confident that the final roundup will still show that the average amount of matter per cubic light-year throughout the space occupied by the local group is at least ten times the average for the rest of surveyed space.

Do the more remote galaxies also belong to groups like our own? Many of them do, perhaps most of them, but some do not. The best way to seek an answer to this question is to examine the distribution of galaxies on the surface of the sky, and also, after estimating their distances, to examine their distribution in space. The survey plates by F. Zwicky and associates at Palomar and by C. D. Shane at the Lick Observatory reveal literally thousands of close groups of galaxies, many of them composed of only a dozen members or less.

We have already seen how difficult and uncertain is the measure of distance to a relatively nearby system like the Andromeda Nebula. The uncertainty of measurement will not decrease as we go farther from home. Nevertheless, with the use of the apparent magnitudes and angular diameters, we shall be able to get a preliminary idea of the distribution of galaxies in distance, as well as on the sky's surface. Then it can be judged whether the ordinary galaxy is isolationist or gregarian.

Census of the Inner Metagalaxy

The catalogue of clusters and nebulae compiled by the Herschels a century ago laid the foundation for J. L. E. Dreyer's *New General Catalogue* which, since its publication in 1888, has been the Holy Writ for astronomers working on nebulae, clusters, and external galaxies. The *New General Catalogue* (NGC) was followed in 1895 and 1910 with the first and second *Index Catalogues* (IC). Altogether the three publications include 13,226 entries. Several hundred numbers have been dropped in the course of later studies because they represented accidental double labeling, or pertained to double or multiple stars mistaken for nebulae. A few, wrongly listed as nebulae, were comets that have long since gone their way.

Many investigators have attempted to sort out the true nebulae from the external galaxies and distinguish the star clusters from everything else; then they make plots and studies of the distribution of the various types of objects catalogued in the NGC and the IC. A number of general conclusions have been correctly drawn from such plots, but the material has always been recognized as inhomogeneous. The Herschelian "sweeps" in the original search for nebulous objects were more complete in some parts of the sky than in others. Here and there the later surveys, using photographic methods, had dipped deep into space and brought up for the catalogues many faint objects in a small area. As a result, the undiscriminating plots of the entries in the NGC and IC occasionally seem to indicate a clustering of galaxies, when the true interpretation is merely depth in the census at that place, or unusual thoroughness.

Recognizing the unevenness of the NGC, the Harvard investigators of star clusters and galaxies undertook some years ago (1930–1932) to employ a uniform series of photographic plates for a preliminary survey of all bright galaxies. For various practical reasons we decided first to make a new homogeneous listing of the galaxies brighter on the photographic scale than the thirteenth magnitude. The catalogue that resulted was published as part 2 of volume 88 of the *Annals of the Harvard College Observatory*.

For the study of what we may call the Inner Metagalaxy this Shapley-Ames catalogue has turned out to be very useful—as useful as it was laborious to prepare. [This same term is used by me in another book, *The Inner Metagalaxy* (Yale University Press, 1957), as a title; it there refers to a much larger volume of space than that involved in the Shapley-Ames catalogue.] The catalogue contains only 1249 galaxies, but two years were required for its formation, even though practically all of the necessary photographic plates were already in existence. The position of every object had to be checked. The photographic magnitude was measured on three plates. Many special sequences of standard stars had to be set up in order to make the magnitude estimates of similar quality over the whole sky. The angular diameters of the galaxies were measured, and something was done with the classifications.

All but 61 of the included objects were already listed half a century before in the NGC (but without useful magnitudes); of these 61 galaxies, 48 were in the IC, and 13 had not heretofore been catalogued. Although the thirteenth photographic magnitude was our desired limit, the catalogue is essentially complete only to magnitude 12.8.

The brightnesses of the galaxies were estimated on small-scale plates made with patrol cameras. On such plates it is possible to

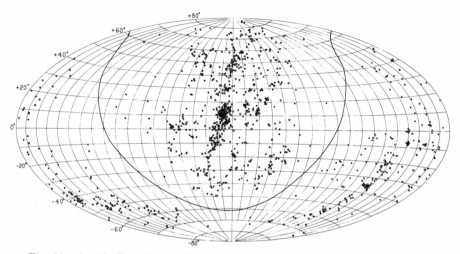

Fig. 64. An Aitoff equal-area chart on which are plotted, for the entire sky, the positions of the thousand brightest galaxies. (From the Shapley-Ames catalogue.)

compare satisfactorily the images of galaxies directly with those of neighboring stars. With a few exceptions they look much alike. Reasonable care was of course exercised in the intercomparisons, and the results turned out to be somewhat better than the observers had expected. Since 1932, when Harvard *Annals 88*, No. 2, was completed, several investigations of some of the magnitudes have been made by more precise methods. Little change has been found necessary, except for the few galaxies brighter than magnitude 10, either in the zero point of the magnitude system or in its scale. If we had attempted to determine the magnitudes of the galaxies on plates made with larger telescopes, we would have gone astray because the stellar images and the nebular images would then have been too dissimilar for accurate estimating. The tiny patrol telescopes did something the giant telescopes could neither do easily, nor accomplish accurately, except through the use of elaborate accessories.

In Figs. 64 and 65 the distribution of the galaxies as shown by the "thirteenth-magnitude" census is illustrated in two different ways. The first figure is the reproduction of an Aitoff "equal-area" chart of the whole sky. Each plotted point represents the position of an external galaxy. The north pole of the heavens (Polaris region) is at the top of the diagram. The middle horizontal line is the celestial equator. The winding curve is the galactic circle, that

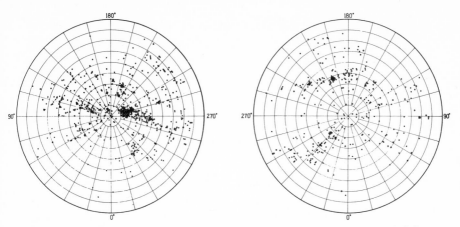

Fig. 65. Another chart of the brighter galaxies, also based on *Harvard College Observatory Annals 88*, No. 2, with separate diagrams for the north (*left*) and south galactic hemispheres. The irregularity in distribution of galaxies is the principal feature of this and the preceding figure.

is, the projection of the mid-line of the Milky Way against the background of the sky.

Two things stand out in this plotting (Fig. 64) of the objects of "*88*, No. 2"—the spottiness of the distribution and the almost complete absence of external galaxies from regions near the galactic circle. The discussion in Chapter 4 tells why galaxies are not seen near the circle, in lowest galactic latitudes. They are simply blocked out, or at least reduced to a magnitude fainter than 13, by the interstellar material near our own galactic plane. Effectively, only about one half of the sky is clear. It is safe to assume that if the dust were absent there would be about twice as many galaxies brighter than the thirteenth magnitude as now appear in our catalogue.

In Fig. 65 the arrangement of these bright galaxies is shown in another kind of diagram—in galactic rather than equatorial coordinates—and the two galactic hemispheres are separated. The material is the same as for Fig. 64. This second aspect of the Inner Metagalaxy again shows the spotted distribution, and the greater richness of the Northern Hemisphere. There are 823 galaxies on the north side of the Milky Way; 426 on the south. The scarcity of the objects around the edges of the plots again emphasizes the effect of space absorption on our survey, for the outer parts of the diagrams correspond to low galactic latitudes.

The charts of distribution do not indicate any strong steady increase in number of galaxies with angular distance from the Milky Way. There is no obvious "concentration toward the galactic poles." If inherently there be such, it is smothered by the conspicuous irregularities in distribution. We shall consider the nonuniformities later, but first let us examine as best we can the distribution of these bright galaxies along the distance coordinate.

It is simple to compute how far the thirteenth-magnitude survey ($m < 12.8$) reaches into space. The distance d in light-years is given by a relation similar to that used in Chapter 2, namely, $\log d = 0.2\,(m - \delta m - M) + 1.5$. If we set $\delta m = 0$, ignoring space absorption for the moment, and then take the absolute magnitude of an *average* galaxy as $M = -16.7$—a currently accepted value, when the objects are selected, as here, on the basis of their apparent brightness—we calculate that the distance of the faintest and most remote *average* galaxy in our catalogue is 25 million light-years.

If all the galaxies were of this average absolute luminosity, we could say that our survey reaches to the calculated distance. But they are not; and the reach is small for dwarfs, greater for giants. For example, dwarf galaxies with $M = -13.7$ would be, when the apparent magnitude is 12.8, at only one-fourth the distance calculated for the average galaxy; all such dwarfs, if between 6 and 25 million light-years distant, would be too faint to get into our thirteenth-magnitude catalogue. On the other hand, giant galaxies of absolute magnitude -18.2 and apparent magnitude 12.8 would be twice as far away as the limiting distance for an average system. In other words, our catalogue contains several giant galaxies that are at a distance of some 50 million light-years, but it is quite incomplete for dwarf galaxies beyond 7 million light-years.

Making some allowances for space absorption, we shall say that *on the average* our bright-galaxy survey covers the first 20 million light-years, except for the low latitudes where we are blacked out by interstellar dust; in those dark regions the survey reaches anywhere from nowhere to nearly 20 million light-years.

While we are considering galaxy distances, it would be well to pause a moment for two incidental observations. The first one relates to units. We find that for the measurement of the Metagalaxy it is as convenient to use the megaparsec for a unit of distance as the light-year. A megaparsec was defined in Chapter 1 as 1 million parsecs, or 3,260,000 light-years. It is the distance at which the radius of the earth's orbit (93 million miles) would subtend an angle of one millionth of a second of arc.

The other digression is to calculate the greatest distance we have now reached with the most powerful telescopes. For this purpose we may work near the galactic poles and assume therefore that space absorption is negligibly small; hence $\delta m = 0$. The faintest external galaxies yet recorded with the largest reflector (the Hale 200-inch telescope on Mount Palomar) are approximately of apparent magnitude $m = 23.0$, after an appropriate correction for red shift. Let us assume, reasonably, that among these faintest objects are some that are absolutely about as bright as the Andromeda Nebula, say $M = -19.5$. The assumption is very reasonable, but we cannot point to any particular image and say that that fuzzy speck records such a supergiant galaxy. We can only say that among a hundred specks at the margin of invisibility the probability is high that a few represent supergiant systems, of absolute magnitude -19.5.

The formula above yields the result:

$$\log d = 0.2 \, (23.0 + 19.5) + 1.5 = 10.0,$$

hence $d = 10,000,000,000$ light-years $= 3,200$ megaparsecs.

We have therefore photographed galaxies in light that has been 100 million centuries crossing about 60,000,000,000,000,000,000,000 miles of space. Such distances are hardly consistent with the evidence of the times involved in the expansion of the universe. How could it get so large at the current rate of expansion during the age we tentatively assign it? The cosmogonic researches of the near future may decide to what depths we have actually reached, and whether the remotest galaxies are as luminous and gigantic as we have supposed.

Let us continue with the consideration of the distribution in distance of the brighter galaxies of the Inner Metagalaxy. We know the position on the sky, that is, the right ascension and declination, of each one of these objects, with high accuracy; but because of the spread in the luminosities of galaxies, some bright, some faint, some average, we cannot easily locate accurately their positions along the line of sight. For a score or so of the nearer ones we can get the distances directly by measuring the brightness of their supergiant stars, when such stars are clearly distinguished. But for the hundreds of others all we can now do is to show, as in Fig. 66, for the material of the Shapley-Ames catalogue, the frequency of the total apparent magnitudes of the galaxies, and say what that frequency indicates about the distances of average galaxies. With space absorption neglected, which is reasonable for the higher galactic latitudes, we can compute that the average galaxy at the eleventh magnitude (the curves indicate about a dozen) would be at a distance of 3.5 megaparsecs; at the twelfth magnitude, 5.7 megaparsecs; at the thirteenth magnitude, 8.3 megaparsecs. (See the formula on p. 54; to get millions of light-years, multiply megaparsecs by 3.26.)

The smooth curve drawn in Fig. 66a indicates what the frequency of the apparent magnitudes would be if the galaxies were distributed with absolute uniformity throughout extragalactic space, that is, if there were no groupings, no systematic increase or decrease of number with distance, but always the same number of galaxies in a given cubic unit of space wherever located. This uniformity assumption, represented by the smooth curve, requires that the number N of galaxies brighter than any given apparent magnitude m is related to that apparent magnitude by the formula

$$\log N = 0.6 \, (m - m_1),$$

where m_1 is a constant called the space-density parameter.

To derive this simple but important formula, which we may call the uniform space-density relation, it is necessary to recall the formal definition of stellar magnitude m as 2.5 times the common logarithm of light intensity l. Numerically, the magnitude increases as the intensity decreases, so that $m \propto \log 1/l$. It is convenient to express the difference between two stellar magnitudes in terms of the ratio of the light intensities:

$$m - m_1 = 2.5 \log l_1/l,$$

and m_1 and l_1 may be taken as standards of magnitude and light intensity to which the other values are referred. Let us proceed to substitute numbers of galaxies for light intensities in this formula, and thus obtain a relation between apparent magnitude and the population of metagalactic space.

Since the intensity of the spreading light varies with the inverse

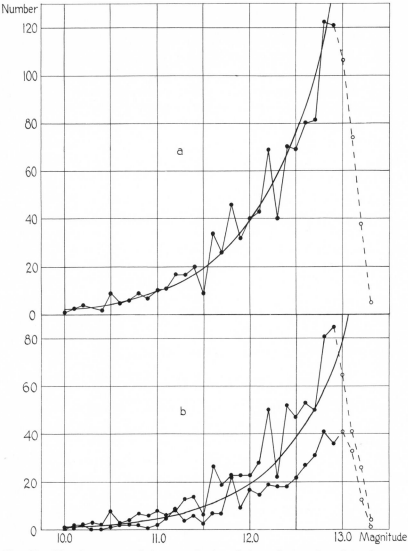

Fig. 66.   The frequency of the magnitudes of the galaxies plotted in the two preceding figures. The vertical coordinates are numbers of galaxies for each tenth of a magnitude. The horizontal coordinates are the apparent photographic magnitudes of the galaxies. The upper figure refers to the whole sky; the lower figure, to the two galactic hemispheres separately, the southern being conspicuously the poorer.

square of the distance d from its source, we have $l \propto 1/d^2$, and

$$l_1/l = d^2/d_1^2.$$

The volume V of the space for which d is the radius (say the volume in metagalactic space of a cone of diameter $1°$ and length d) varies, of course, with the cube of d, and therefore $d \propto V^{1/3}$ and

$$l_1/l = d^2/d_1^2 = V^{2/3}/V_1^{2/3}.$$

Therefore

$$2.5 \log V^{2/3}/V_1^{2/3} = m - m_1$$

or

$$\log V/V_1 = 0.6 \, (m - m_1).$$

If space is uniformly populated with galaxies, their number N must increase with distance exactly as the volume of space increases with distance. Therefore $V/N = V_1/N_1$, where V_1 and N_1 may be taken as referring to the space defined by d_1 and l_1. Accordingly, we can write

$$\log N/N_1 = 0.6 \, (m - m_1).$$

If the standard limit m_1 of a "standard" survey of galaxies is so chosen that it corresponds to a distance d_1 and volume V_1 that are large enough to include just one galaxy, then $N_1 = 1$, and we have

$$\log N = 0.6 \, (m - m_1),$$

a formula that will be much used in our work of relating the number of galaxies to the apparent magnitude of the limit reached in various statistical surveys.

In practice it is found convenient to choose the unit volume as that covered by only 1 square degree of the sky. Therefore m_1 must be very faint in order to provide sufficient depth and volume to include on the average one average galaxy. The photographic magnitude 15.2, we shall see later, seems to be a good mean value of m_1, the space-density parameter, for the sky at large.

The space-density relation holds, by the way, even when there is a diversity among the actual luminosities of the galaxies, provided that the spread in the luminosities—that is, the relative numbers of dwarfs, normals, giants—is the same in all parts of the space considered. The formula is interpreted further in Chapter 7.

At first sight the deviation from uniformity seems not large. The smooth curve in Fig. 66a fits fairly well. But this is accidental, for in Fig. 66b, where the Northern and Southern Hemispheres are treated separately, the agreement is poor between observation and the uniformity curve. A clumpiness in the distribution of galaxies is suggested. Moreover, the surface distribution (Figs. 64 and 65) also emphasizes the grouping that prevails in some regions. Because of its significance in cosmogony, we shall presently give further attention to the phenomenon of galaxy clustering, but first a look at the seemingly uninhabited celestial desert along the Milky Way —a desert for galaxies, even though it is the dominating metropolis for stars, nebulae, star clusters, and dust. This celestial Sahara is indeed so dusty that not only the galaxies but a majority of the remote Milky Way stars are dimmed out of our visual and photographic reach. The radio telescopes do a better job of penetrating dust clouds than either the human eye or the photographic plate.

The Region of Avoidance

The most pronounced unevenness in the distribution of galaxies is the rich population in high latitudes contrasted with the low population near the galactic circle. The region so conspicuously "avoided" by the galaxies, known to workers in this field for a century, was pointed out most clearly by Richard A. Proctor some 90 years ago through his plotting of the objects recorded in Sir John Herschel's "General Catalogue." One of his illustrations is reproduced in Fig. 67.

The analogous, but much narrower, "region of avoidance" that pertains to globular star clusters of the galactic system was referred to in Chapter 4. It is now accepted that the narrow zone for clusters and the wide one for external galaxies arise from the same general cause—space absorption blocking out a part of the population. Region of obscuration would be a better name.

Miss Jacqueline Sweeney and I have made a special survey, on 400 long-exposure plates, of the distribution of 60,000 southern faint galaxies to show the extent of the light blocking in the southern Milky Way. The results are summarized in Fig. 85 in Chapter 7.

The region of obscuration for external galaxies is also shown by Hubble's sample-areas survey with the Mount Wilson reflectors (Fig. 68). His surveys, like those carried on at Harvard, not only reveal regions where the light of distant galaxies is completely blocked, but near the borders of the Milky Way they also help to

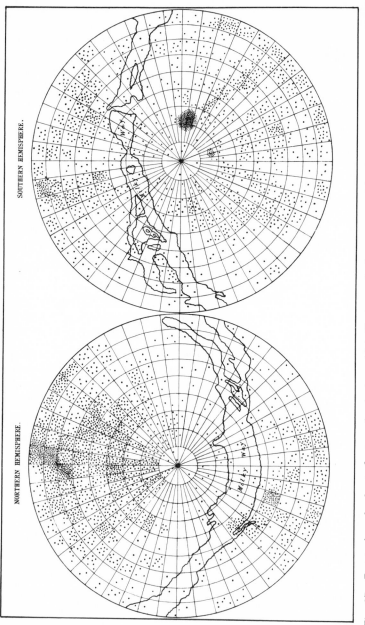

Fig. 67. Proctor's early chart of external galaxies, which illustrates the important region of avoidance. The circular groups near the center of the right-hand figure represent nebulae and clusters in the two Magellanic Clouds. At the top of the left-hand figure is located the rich cloud of galaxies in Virgo.

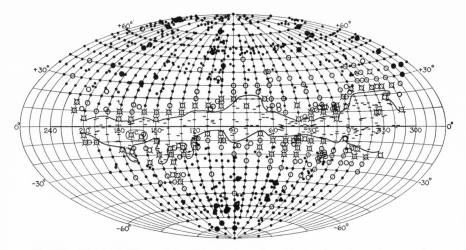

Fig. 68. Hubble's illustration of the region of avoidance, based on photographs taken with the Mount Wilson reflectors.

measure quantitatively the amount of the absorption of light in space.

When we work in regions 30° or more from the Milky Way, we can, in the first approximation, ignore the space absorption. Certainly that is possible within 50° of the galactic poles, since the actual irregularities in the distribution of galaxies in the higher latitudes (Fig. 65) tend to conceal the evidence for whatever space absorption there may be in those regions.

The Virgo Cluster of Galaxies

The most conspicuous clustering shown in our thirteenth-magnitude survey is the one centered near right ascension 12^h 30^m, declination $+12°$. This group lies chiefly in the constellation Virgo. There is also a considerable but looser grouping north of the Virgo cluster, extending about 40° through Coma, Lynx, and Ursa Major. In an analysis of the distribution of galaxies brighter than magnitude 12.7 (more than half of those in the Shapley-Ames catalogue), Katz and Mulders have shown that the chance is only one in 420 million that the arrangement of galaxies is random. In other words, the clustering is emphatically genuine. In the other hemisphere there is a bright group in Fornax, and there are others in Dorado and Grus. The Virgo organization merits a brief description since its relative nearness makes it particularly suitable for exploration.

Position and Population. It has been fortunate for astronomers, and for those who learn from them, that a supersystem of galaxies, much richer than our local group, is situated in a region favorable for detailed investigation. The Virgo cluster is near enough the celestial equator to be conveniently studied from all the important observatories, north and south. It is far enough from the galactic equator, with its troublesome space absorption, to simplify somewhat the photometry, as well as the measurement of distance. According to E. Holmberg, it appears to be about 11 megaparsecs away—a neighborly system as far as clusters of galaxies go, since its members are within range of both moderate-sized visual telescopes and small photographic cameras.

The diagram in Fig. 69 shows how the hundred brightest members

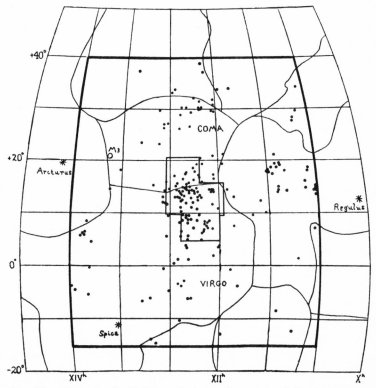

Fig. 69. The Virgo cloud of bright galaxies at the center of the Arcturus-Spica-Regulus triangle.

of the Virgo group stand out when all galaxies brighter than the thirteenth magnitude are plotted for that part of the sky. The center of the concentration is near the middle of the triangle formed by the conspicuous stars Regulus, Spica, and Arcturus. No member of the group is visible to our unaided eyes, because the more than 35 million light-years of intervening space has attenuated the light so that even the giant galaxies of the group can be seen only with the aid of a telescope.

When we extend our survey of the Virgo group to its fainter galaxies—to the fifteenth magnitude, for instance—we nearly double the population assignable to the cluster. It is difficult, however, to disentangle these fainter cluster members from the population of the general metagalactic field.

Galaxy Types, Resolution, and Relative Sizes. Much attention has been paid to the Virgo group of galaxies, especially at the Mount Wilson, Palomar, and Harvard observatories. We know that about three-fourths of the bright members are spirals, and the others are mostly spheroidal. There are but a few of the irregular Magellanic type among the brighter galaxies. An occasional spiral is somewhat freakish, but the majority belong to the category that we call *Sc*. At the Palomar Observatory a considerable number of these *Sc* spirals have been resolved; that is, individual supergiant stars within each galaxy, and clusters of giant stars, have been segregated, and their magnitudes estimated. Eventually all the *Sc* objects, from about magnitude 10.5 to 15, may be resolved, and also most of the *Sb* spirals.

The *Sa* spirals and the spheroidal galaxies are more difficult to resolve, not so much because of the compactness of structure as because supergiant stars are infrequent if not completely absent. Their ordinary giant stars, and of course the average stars like our sun, are too faint for the telescopic power of the present or near future. The brightest Magellanic-type systems would be easily resolvable if they were present in the Virgo cloud, for they, like our own Magellanic Clouds, would presumably be rich in supergiant stars. Among the dwarf members of the Virgo Cloud are many irregular galaxies that have been identified on Lick and Palomar photographs; they are too faint for the bright-galaxy catalogue.

It is of interest that throughout this Virgo assemblage, from brightest to the fifteenth magnitude, the relative numbers of spheroidal and spiral galaxies remain about the same. Also at any given brightness the over-all dimensions of the individual galaxies are found to be much alike for all galaxy types when the photographic exposures are sufficiently prolonged to reveal the faint outer portions of the spheroidal galaxies. The significance of this observational fact is noted later in the present chapter and in the next.

Speeds and Masses. The radial velocities of about 100 of the Virgo galaxies have been measured, mostly by Humason at the Mount Wilson and Palomar Observatories. The group *as a whole* shows a recession from our Galaxy of the order of 700 miles per second; but there is much motion within the cluster, with a spread of more than 1600 miles per second in the velocities of the individual members.

Making use of the velocities, with certain assumptions concerning their meaning, Sinclair Smith has calculated what the total mass of the Virgo organization must be. It is enormous; and, when divided among the individual members now recorded, it indicates that they are each the equivalent of about 200,000 million suns. This seems like far too much mass for the amount of light produced, which averages but a few hundred million sun-power per galaxy. An alternative to accepting the great individual masses is to assume that much of the matter of the Virgo cluster is nonluminous dust in the spaces between galaxies. Or perhaps the speedy internal motions should not be attributed wholly to the gravitational interaction of the individual galaxies, and should not therefore be taken as indicators of great mass. Further observation and further analysis are both important.

Spectral Types and Colors. The average spectral class of the Virgo galaxies, and of almost all others that have been sufficiently investigated, is near that of the sun, *G*0. Some are of Class *F,* most are of Class *G.* Many of the irregular and *Sc* galaxies have spectral peculiarities that probably indicate the presence within them of very bright nebulae, or of groups of hot blue stars. They are the "blue" galaxies under investigation by G. Haro at Tonanzintla, and are importantly involved in W. W. Morgan's new classification. It should be noted that a composite of all ordinary classes of stars, *O, B, A, F, G, K, M, N,* would be something like Class *G.*

The colors of galaxies have been measured by Stebbins and Whitford, Whipple, Seyfert, Haro, and others, with the uniform result that the color is about what one would expect it to be, considering the spectra, if there is no serious reddening of light in space. The colors, in fact, indicate high space transparency in the direction of the Virgo cluster, and perhaps they also indicate that there is not much space absorption within the Virgo cloud itself.

The Spiral Arms. In a detailed study of the distribution of the light throughout many of the spiral and spheroidal galaxies of the Virgo cluster, Miss Shirley Patterson has made a significant contribution. The results of some of her work are illustrated in Figs. 70 and 71. The investigation is intended to yield clues to the internal structure of large stellar systems, a subject to which Oort in Holland, Lindblad and Holmberg in Sweden, and Hubble and Randers in America, among others, have also given much attention.

We do not yet understand fully the spiral structure, which appears to dominate more than two-thirds of all bright galaxies in the Virgo cluster. The problem may be one of the most basic, as it is certainly one of the most difficult, in galactic mechanics. Perhaps the study of the motions in our own Galaxy will help to solve the problem for the spirals; or the solution for the spirals may aid in untangling the puzzles in our own Galaxy. Miss Patterson's photographs, made with a specially suitable telescope at the Agassiz station of the Harvard Observatory, when analyzed with the aid of a microdensitometer, bring out the important point that not much more than

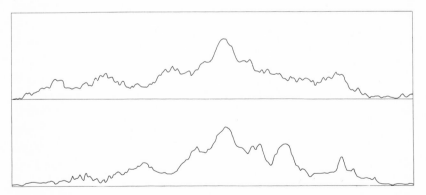

Fig. 70. Microdensitometer tracings from an Agassiz Station photograph of the spiral Messier 101. (See also Fig. 54.) The two tracings cross the nucleus and the spiral-arm structure north to south (*top*) and east to west (*bottom*), and both record spiral arms in the guise of humps in the tracings. The vertical coordinate is a measure of density on the photographic plate, and therefore represents brightness in the galaxy.

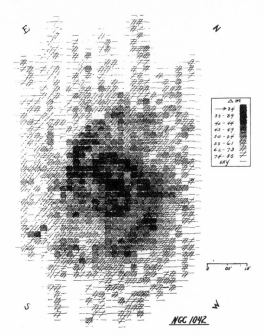

Fig. 71. A microdensitometer analysis of a face-on spiral by Miss F. S. Patterson, working on a photograph made with the 12-inch Metcalf refractor at Oak Ridge. The plot of the photometric measures clearly reproduces the spiral arms.

20 percent (frequently less) of the light of the spiral galaxy comes from the spiral arms. There is a great deal of light under and between the arms, which have been overemphasized, perhaps because by contrast they do stand out from the amorphous background. As noted previously, the diameters of spiral and spheroidal galaxies in Virgo are about the same. Also galaxies of both types extend much farther from their nuclei than the early photographs indicated. It is probable that the material of the arms is not ejected from the nucleus, as formerly supposed, but rather represents a condensation or concentration superposed on the smooth background of a discoid of unresolved stars. Dust and gas are involved in the spiral structure, and we now believe that the supergiant bluish stars of the arms are being currently born of the dust and gas and are destined to live brilliant fast-fading lives.

The motion of the material in the arms is critical in the dynamical problems of the galaxies. Hubble and Mayall have made observations that appear to confirm definitely the early conclusion of V. M. Slipher that a rotating spiral trails its arms behind it. Lindblad finds some evidence for preceding arms, and even of following and preceding arms in the same rotating system.

Remark on Freaks. One feature of the spiral category that may be both an obstacle and a blessing in the interpretation of galaxies is the frequent appearance of abnormality, both in the armed structure and in the nuclei. In the first chapter we have called attention to the barred spiral, with its subdivisions. There are also plate spirals, and frankly "pathological" types (as Baade called such freaks) like NGC 5128 (Fig. 83) and the ring-tail systems, NGC 4038–9 and 4027, shown in Fig. 72. Many double galaxies have connecting streams of

Fig. 72. The ring-tail galaxy is a rare type of external system; but, strange to say, the two brightest are separated in the sky by less than 1 degree. They are NGC 4038–9 (*upper corner*) and NGC 4027. (Harvard photograph, Bruce telescope.)

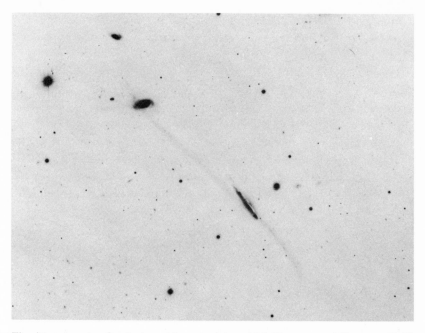

Fig. 73. A pair of galaxies with connecting tidal filament and "countertidal" streamer. (Palomar photograph, 200-inch telescope.)

light—some streams apparently composed of stars, some of dust and gas. Zwicky, Page, Carpenter, and Holmberg are workers in this important field.

Theories that sufficiently explain a relatively simple-looking *Sc* spiral, like Messier 33 and the most common galaxies in Virgo, must have sufficient flexibility to take care of these aberrant types. The interpreter may need to resort to the assumption of collisions to find satisfactory causes. He would have some justification, since encounters may have been fairly frequent in the remote past (see Fig. 73). Or as an explanation of deviation from normality he may resort to postulating uncommon conditions at birth. We are only at the doorstep of the house of galactic knowledge, and within there are doubtless many dark and difficult rooms to explore and set in order.

Are We in the Virgo Cloud? Returning to the diagrams showing the location of the Virgo cluster of galaxies (Fig. 64, 65, and 69), we notice that south of the main body of the cluster is an extension running nearly 30° toward the constellation Centaurus. Is this a part

Fig. 74.   A company of three tilted spirals in the far south, NGC 7582, 7590, 7599. (Harvard photograph, Bruce telescope.)

of the Virgo supersystem? If so, the over-all length is more than 8 million light-years. And to the northward are scattered bright galaxies, many of the same brightness and probably at about the same distance from us as the members of the cluster of galaxies in Virgo. Are they part of the same physical system? We should perhaps question, as Zwicky, de Vaucouleurs, and others have done, whether we ourselves are not a part of this great cloud of galaxies that has a small condensation near us—the local family— as well as the much richer condensation in Virgo and the string of galaxies south and north. A local supergalaxy is suggested.

Evidence is growing that a large proportion of the galaxies within 40 million light-years are not free individuals in the metagalactic field, but rather are members of loose groups (Fig. 74). Are these sparse groups dissolving, or forming? We must wait and see. A billion years should suffice, or much less if our mathematical analyses of space, time, matter, and motion prosper.

The Fornax Group of Galaxies, and Others

Table 4 lists some of the information we have at hand concerning a score of bright objects in the constellation Fornax, which are so located with respect to one another that the law of chance is hard

TABLE 4. *Bright galaxies in Fornax.*

NGC number	Type	Magnitude	Right ascension	Declination
1316	Spheroidal	10.1	3^h $20^m.7$	$-37°$ $25'$
1317	Spiral	12.2	3 20.8	-37 17
1326	Barred spiral	11.8	3 22.0	-36 39
1350	Barred spiral	11.8	3 29.1	-33 38
1351	Spheroidal	12.8	3 28.6	-35 2
1365	Barred spiral	11.2	3 31.8	-36 18
1374	Spheroidal	12.4	3 33.4	-35 24
1379	Spheroidal	12.3	3 34.2	-35 37
1380	Spiral	11.4	3 34.6	-35 0
1381	Spiral	12.6	3 34.7	-35 28
1386	Barred spiral	12.4	3 35.0	-36 10
1387	Spheroidal	12.1	3 35.1	-35 41
1389	Spheroidal	12.8	3 35.3	-35 55
1399	Spheroidal	10.9	3 36.6	-35 37
1404	Spheroidal	11.5	3 37.0	-35 45
1427	Spheroidal	12.4	3 40.4	-35 34
1437	Spiral	12.9	3 41.7	-36 1

pressed if these objects are only accidentally near together. They appear to constitute a real colony of galaxies, mutually operating. In a number of groups such as this one we find that the brightest galaxy is of the spheroidal type. Here it is the strongly concentrated NGC 1316. But, as mentioned above in Chapter 5, there are also in the Fornax group dwarf spheroidals, similar to the unusual galaxy in Sculptor, which is one of the dwarf members of our own small family of galaxies. If the dwarf Sculptor galaxy were at the distance of the giant NGC 1316, and alongside it, the contrast would be most striking.

This contrast in luminosity emphasizes the fact that in our examination of the various groups of external galaxies, near or distant, we are always exposed to bias because we most easily study the giant galaxies. Our census of the population of a cluster of galaxies may be complete for the bright and sometimes for the intermediate objects, but in no group but our own do we yet know much about dwarf or subdwarf systems. We merely accept their probable abundance, and ignore them, as in the following paragraphs on clusters of galaxies.

Fortunately there seems to be fair evidence that the spread of luminosities in groups of galaxies does not often exceed six magnitudes, and that the most frequent galaxy in a cluster is only three magnitudes fainter than the brightest member of the system. The faintest dwarfs are about the same amount fainter than the average. Such a spread is approximately true in the Virgo cluster—nearly true, in fact, in our local cluster of galaxies, where only our galactic system and the Andromeda Nebula appear gigantic.

To the extent that we can trust this preliminary evidence of a six-magnitude spread, we can estimate the relative distance of a fairly rich cluster of galaxies, with average or "statistical" success, from the photometry of only the brightest few members which we easily see and measure. Poor groups of galaxies, like the Fornax clustering, cannot be measured trustworthily by this simple procedure. But for the more populous groups we simply estimate the apparent magnitudes of the brightest objects in the cluster of galaxies, estimate also the correction necessary for space absorption, and assume, of course, that the absolute magnitudes of the galaxies, and the spread thereof, are normal. Since the absolute magnitude of the average galaxy is about -15.7, the brightest of all in a rich cluster of galaxies is close to $M = -19$. We can therefore use the apparent magnitude m as an indicator of distance, since all we need to know is the modulus $m - M$.

The fifth galaxy from the top averages about -18.5, and this fifth galaxy, rather than the first, provides a somewhat more reliable estimate for the distance of a rich cluster of galaxies, much as the fifth brightest star provides similarly for estimating the distance of a globular star cluster. In both places the error introduced by an accidentally superposed bright object is lessened by using as a standard the fifth from the top rather than the brightest; the fifth has greater statistical reliability.

It turns out that from measures of apparent brightness only, and from the knowledge and techniques derived from studies of clusters of stars and clusters of galaxies, we can for the latter determine distances up to 200 million light-years and more, and know something of the error of the estimates. The error is not discouragingly large until we get out so far and so faint that we encounter the grave uncertainties (1) in the magnitude scales, (2) in the correction for the red shift, and (3) in the correction for space curvature, if any.

Thousands of clusters of galaxies are now known to be as rich as the nearby Virgo system, or richer. On plates made with the Palomar 48-inch Schmidt telescope G. O. Abell has indentified 2712 such clusters of galaxies. There are tens of thousands of groups that are as populous as the local group of galaxies, and also thousands of large distributional irregularities that strongly suggest immense physical associations. We observe, in fact, a basic tendency to cluster, whichever way we turn, and a high frequency of doubles. One is reminded of stellar analogies in our own Galaxy, where we find organizations of stars running from doubles through all degrees of grouping up to the myriad-starred globular clusters.

Faint-Galaxy Surveys at Harvard, Mount Wilson, Palomar, and Lick Observatories

The usefulness of the thirteenth-magnitude survey tempted the Harvard galaxy investigators to make a more far-reaching census. It seemed to be within reason to go to the eighteenth magnitude— not so deep that the galaxies, which come at the rate of one every cubic million light-years or so, would be practically innumerable, but deep enough that the returns should provide a large body of material—more than half a million galaxies (see Fig. 75)—for the examination of such cosmic problems as:

(1) The nature of the deviations from uniformity in the distribution of galaxies throughout the surrounding volume of space that has a radius of 200 or 300 million light-years;

(2) Statistics on the clustering of galaxies, and the bearing of such clusters on the development of the Metagalaxy;

(3) The distribution of light-absorbing material in our own Galaxy, as indicated by the visibility of external galaxies along the Milky Way borders;

(4) The mean density of matter in explorable extragalactic space;

(5) The existence of significant large-scale gradients in the galaxy population of the space explored.

The survey covers the whole sky. The photographs for the Southern Hemisphere were made with the 24-inch Bruce refractor, located on Harvard Kopje, near Bloemfontein, South Africa. The survey in the northern sky is based on plates made with the 16-inch Metcalf refractor, located at the Agassiz station on Oak Ridge, 25 miles northwest of Cambridge, Massachusetts. These instruments are of the same kind. They could be much improved with new-type lenses, but at the time of the census they were the two best galaxy-

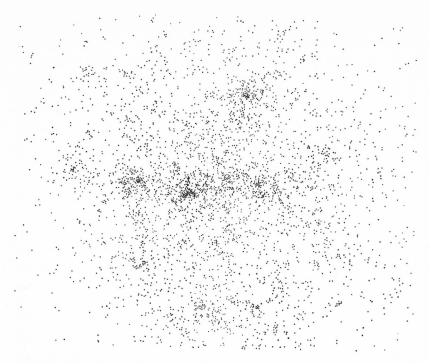

Fig. 75.   This plot, made from a 3-hour-exposure photograph with the Bruce doublet at the Boyden Station, shows the distribution of 4000 galaxies heretofore unrecorded. The field center is at R.A. 13^h 25^m, Dec. $-31°$.

recording instruments (for survey work) in their respective hemispheres. Although they penetrated less deeply than the larger reflecting telescopes, they had the decided advantage in survey work of covering large fields. They each photographed satisfactorily something like 30 square degrees at a time, whereas the typical large reflector handles but a fraction of a single degree on one photograph. In 3-hour exposures on fast plates the Harvard instruments record stars somewhat fainter than the eighteenth magnitude —hence the name of the survey. But the galaxies are photographed satisfactorily for discovery only if they are as bright as stars that are approximately half a magnitude above the plate limit. The "eighteenth-magnitude survey," therefore, does not include all the galaxies to the eighteenth magnitude; magnitude 17.6 is approximately the limit for completeness.

More than half of the sky has been examined on the long-exposure Harvard plates. Six hundred thousand new galaxies have been marked for the metagalactic census, and magnitudes for tens of thousands have been measured.

Deeper than this eighteenth-magnitude survey have gone some of the sample-area countings by Hubble, who used the Mount Wilson reflectors. Long-exposure plates with the 100-inch telescope have reached to the twentieth magnitude and fainter. Hubble photographed areas so chosen as to give at least preliminary information concerning the nebular population throughout all the space within easy reach of that instrument. The total number of galaxies photographed in such a sample-area survey is of course small compared with the total take by the sky-covering Bruce and Metcalf telescopes. The two types of survey are, however, complementary; and the pictures they give us of the Metagalaxy are mutually consistent. They agree in showing that more than a billion galaxies are within the distance explorable by the greatest telescopes, but nearly half of these galaxies are concealed by low-latitude obscuration.

Two new surveys are adding importantly to our knowledge of what we may still call the inner Metagalaxy. One is the work of the 20-inch Carnegie astrograph at the Lick Observatory, and the other is the survey with the Schmidt 48-inch reflector on Mount Palomar. The former will involve about twice as many galaxies as are recorded in Harvard's "eighteenth-magnitude" program, and the latter perhaps five times as many; neither covers the southernmost quarter of the sky.

Toward what revelations of knowledge and ignorance these current explorations of the Metagalaxy are leading will be indicated in the chapter that follows.

7

The Expanding Universe

The mystery of the origin, destiny, and meaning of the physical universe inevitably incites to meditation all those who enter the spaces and times of the Metagalaxy. Whence did it come; whither is it going—and what is man that he writes books about it, and reads them? Certainly self-interest flavors his meditation, for, as the galaxies go, so go the stars and the sun, and the sun's third planet earth with its superficial biology. But in this concluding chapter we shall evade the basic *hows* and *whys,* and continue to present the fragmentary observations and explanations that are slowly leading toward a finished picture of the sidereal world.

In entitling this chapter "The Expanding

Universe," we have in mind, of course, the widely known observation that galaxies appear to recede from one another. If some day it should be convincingly shown that the red shift can be satisfactorily explained without recourse to the theory of a physical expansion of the Metagalaxy, then the title above, we could say, refers to the unquestionable expansion of the universe of knowledge about the universe. Not only is that informational expansion unquestioned, it is amazing. The universe of galaxies is expanding at a rate that doubles the radius of a few thousand million years; but our knowledge of the universe doubles in one human generation. Our accelerated understanding encompasses not only galaxies and the anatomy of stars, but also the minutest particles, and their behavior in the microcosmos of molecules, atoms, and photons.

The machinery for research, in nearly all scientific fields, rapidly expands in variety and efficiency. New techniques evolve each year. Much inspiring accomplishment appears to be within our grasp. It will indeed be just as interesting to see how far human skill and understanding can go in this universe as to see what happens to colliding galaxies, exploding supernovae, dissolving comets, and dying radiation.

The Space-Density Parameter

When we finished the preceding chapter we were 200 million light-years distant among the eighteenth-magnitude galaxies. It will be instructive to examine in some detail a sample of this metagalactic realm.

The distribution of the faint galaxies over the central 9 square degrees of an average high-latitude Bruce plate, No. 20,309, of 3 hours' exposure, is shown in Fig. 76. The 659 small arrowheads point to the positions where an eyepiece examination of the original negative has shown new galaxies, heretofore unrecorded in any catalogue, probably never photographed before this plate was made. The large arrowheads locate the three external galaxies that had been recorded previously. They were, in fact, catalogued in the NGC and are conspicuous enough to be seen on this reproduction, although most of the fainter objects are lost in the process of reproducing.

The faint objects found on the plate are of various apparent magnitudes. In Fig. 77 is a diagram of the magnitude distribution.

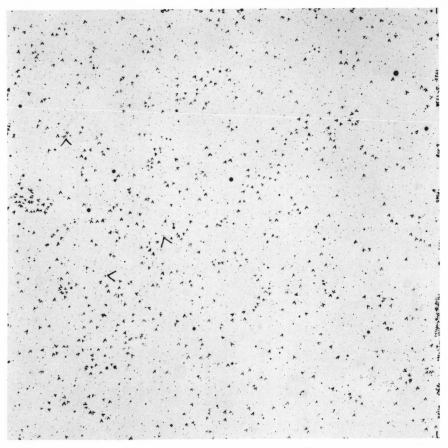

Fig. 76.   The central 9 square degrees of a Bruce plate of 3 hours' exposure, with large arrows indicating the 3 previously known galaxies and small arrows marking the 659 faint ones that now come into the census of the Metagalaxy.

The vertical ordinates are numbers of galaxies in each small interval of brightness; the abscissas are the magnitudes. It is a conventional plot of the yield of galaxies as photographically we reach deeper into the Metagalaxy. Magnitude 17.9 is the limit to which the galaxy count on this plate is complete.

If space were uniformly populated with galaxies in the direction we have photographed on No. 20,309, the distribution would be as shown by the curved line. Obviously the fit of the actual count of galaxies to the uniformity hypothesis is not very good. There is an excess of galaxies around the eighteenth magnitude and a small deficiency around magnitude 16.5. The rise in the population graph

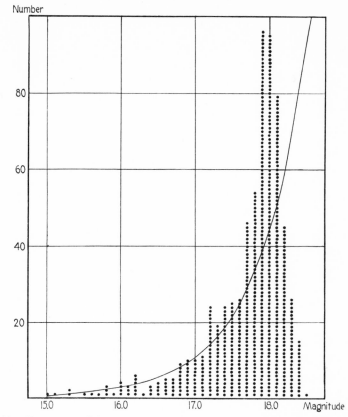

Fig. 77. Frequency of the apparent magnitudes of the newly recorded galaxies of Fig. 76.

is too steep for the uniformity hypothesis beyond magnitude 17.0. We may have reached into a metagalactic cloud of galaxies at a distance of about 100 megaparsecs. That would account for the excess, and the steepness. Another possibility, but not probability, is that the magnitude standards are at fault.

To explain more technically in two paragraphs the practical procedure in this probing of space, let us plot as ordinate the logarithms of the numbers of galaxies brighter than a given magnitude, and not, as in Fig. 77, the numbers themselves. We get the diagram in Fig. 78. The straight line through the plotted points is the best representation we can obtain. It represents uniformity (the uniformity relation is derived and explained in the preceding chapter). The equation of the line may be written

$$\log N = b(m - m_1),$$

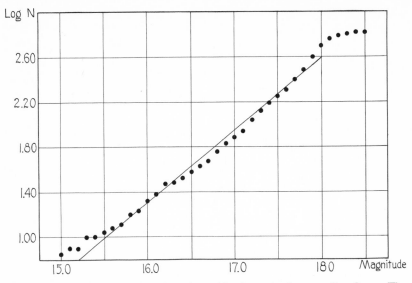

Fig. 78. Logarithmic plot, based on the results shown in the preceding figure. The slope of the line is important in the study of the population of space.

where N is the number of galaxies per square degree down to a given apparent magnitude m, and b and m_1 are constants defining, respectively, the slope of the line and its zero point. Ordinarily we call b the coefficient of the density gradient, and m_1 the space-density parameter. The latter is the magnitude down to which the survey must reach—here it is 13.9 for all 9 square degrees, or 15.5 for 1 square degree—in order to find on the average *one* galaxy per square degree. To check this definition, note that when $m = m_1$ the right-hand member of the equation becomes zero, and therefore N becomes unity. We determine m simply by counting galaxies of measured magnitude; but measuring the magnitudes accurately is not simple. If space is far from uniformly populated, the quantity m_1 has only local meaning and is not cosmically significant.

To illustrate the operation of the foregoing relation, let us suppose that there is at least approximate uniformity in the space distribution of galaxies, and therefore $b = 0.6$. Then, if we find on the average 1 galaxy per square degree by going down to magnitude 15.5, as we do for Bruce plate No. 20309, we should find on the average 4 when we get down to magnitude 16.5, 16 down to magnitude 17.5, and so on. Going in the other direction, it should require 4 square degrees to produce one galaxy of magnitude 14.5 or brighter, and 2048 square degrees (227 plates) (with the average population shown in Fig. 76) to have 1 galaxy of the tenth magnitude or brighter. Since 2048 square degrees is about 5 percent of the whole sky, we can compute from the faint-galaxy count on this one plate that there are all over the sky about 10 to 12 galaxies brighter than the tenth magnitude (allowing for dimming by interstellar dust)—and this number is not far wrong by actual bright-galaxy count, which gives 20.

For the Bruce plate represented by Fig. 76, the density-gradient coefficient is $b = 0.66$. If the coefficient b were exactly 0.6, the density of galaxies in space, in the direction covered by this photograph, would be exactly uniform; that is, every unit of volume of metagalactic space would contain the same number of galaxies and matter would be uniformly distributed (in galaxy-sized chunks) throughout the space covered by the magnitude survey.

Since the density parameter m_1 really defines the number of average-sized galaxies in a unit volume of space, it is an important quantity, because its numerical value has much to do with the facts of cosmogony—with the interpretation of the nature of space-time, the age of the expanding universe, and other questions of this sort. For example, its average numerical value is about 15.2; but if m_1 were 14.2, there would be four times as many galaxies in a given volume of space, the space-density of matter would be correspondingly four times greater, and the scattering of galaxies would be considerably less advanced than we now find it.

Anticipating the arguments of a later section, we note that the smaller the quantity m_1, the "younger" the expansion; the greater this parameter, the further along we are in our approach to zero density and infinite dissipation. Since galaxies are receding, and growing dimmer, m_1 increases with time. Some day, billions of years from now, m_1 will be fainter than magnitude 27, and it may then be difficult to photograph more than a score of galaxies, whereas now we can catalogue millions.

We are not quite ready to use the space-density parameter freely in cosmic interpretations because of suspected changes in its value from point to point in space, and especially because of the fog we are in with respect to the masses of individual galactic systems. We cannot yet say that so many galaxies per average cubic megaparsec means exactly so many grams of matter per average cubic centimeter. We do not as yet know how many stars or grams of matter the average galaxy contains. It is therefore still an uncertain leap from the number of galaxies per unit volume to the average density of matter in space. A fair estimate of average density is 10^{-30} gm/cm^3, or, in words, approximately a thousandth of a millionth of a billionth of a trillionth of the density of water.

Density Gradients

Is there any evidence of a center of the Metagalaxy? Any evidence of an edge? Do our observations show any tendency toward systematic concentration, or systematic thinning out, in the number of galaxies, in the amount of matter, as we move in million-light-year strides across metagalactic space?

We have found many cases of irregularities in the distribution of galaxies, but is there a general trend that would suggest a form or structure of the Metagalaxy similar to that of a star cluster with dense nucleus and peripheral thinness, or analogous to the structure of our flattened-spiral Galaxy?

To save time, we go to the answer immediately, without bothering to present facts or arguments. The answer is, "No bottom." There is no indication of a boundary; nor is there good evidence that there might not be one if we went out far enough. If our measuring rods were longer than a billion light-years, or more sensitive to small density changes, we might find a falling off in some direction, or a clear trend toward some all-dominating nuclear cloud of galaxies; or we might glimpse clear evidence for a finite curved space; or, more likely, we might find as now no bottom and no excessive variation in the average frequency of galaxies.

The edge structure, if any, of the metagalactic system appears to escape us, but there is increasing knowledge of the internal anatomy. Already we have noted the giants and the dwarfs and the many types among the galaxies. We have photographed doubles, triples, multiples of many sorts. Thousands of groups are on record, and not a few very rich clusters of galaxies. In other words, we find not a rigorous identity among galaxies and not a dead uniformity in their distribution, but a prevalence of vestigial or embryonic organizations. We also find large clouds of galaxies of irregular outline—clouds that suggest chaos rather than orderliness. Certainly much time must flow before we attain, if ever, a smoothly populated Metagalaxy.

When we find great unevenness in the distribution of galaxies in low latitudes, we may resort for the explanation to the hypothesis of light-scattering material in the interstellar spaces of our own Galaxy. But in many high-latitude regions we also find conspicuous irregularities in distribution that cannot well be attributed to clouds of intervening dust. We accept them as large-scale irregularities in metagalactic structure.

Figure 64 in Chapter 6 illustrates nonuniformity for the galaxies within 30 million light-years. As mentioned earlier, a number of other large-scale nonuniformities, larger than clusters of galaxies, have been found within the space now explorable. Long ago, for instance, it was noticed that the sky is much richer in bright galaxies in the northern galactic hemisphere (Virgo, Coma, Bootes, Ursa Major, Canes Venatici, and other constellations) than in the opposite southern galactic hemisphere (Pisces, Cetus, Sculptor, Aquarius, Pegasus, and others). Some investigators have taken the difference in the observed frequency of galaxies in the two hemispheres to be the result of the scattering and absorption of light within our galactic system. They argue that the number of recorded galaxies is greater on the north side because the sun is slightly to the north of the galactic plane, and therefore nearer the northern boundary of the supposedly uniform layer of scattering dust. There are several objections to this simple interpretation of the asymmetry in distribution. One is the lack of supporting evidence from the colors of stars and galaxies, although that objection could be met by "protective" subhypotheses. Another is the insufficiency of the absorption hypothesis, since the still greater differences in numbers of galaxies from one region to another in one and the same hemisphere remain unexplained. But the distributional inequalities for bright galaxies, and with them the absorption-inequality hypothesis, disappear in the more recent Harvard and Mount Wilson faint-galaxy surveys, for at the eighteenth magnitude and fainter the galaxies appear to be equally numerous in the two hemispheres.

The observed difference between the north and south galactic hemispheres in the numbers of galaxies at the thirteenth magnitude (Fig. 65) is therefore only a structural detail of the Inner Metagalaxy. The rich cluster of galaxies in Virgo contributes much to this inequality; but it persists even when we disallow the contribution from that prominent organization.

Some time ago I undertook to examine quantitatively this north-south inequality, which is so conspicuous at the twelfth and thirteenth magnitudes, and apparently absent at the twentieth. The question of inequality for intermediate magnitudes and distances was examined. Galaxy counts were carried out in twelve high-latitude fields in the north and twelve in the south. Between the sixteenth and eighteenth magnitudes the values of the ratio of northern to southern galaxies (in half-magnitude intervals) were found to be as follows:

Magnitude	16.0	16.1	16.6	17.1	17.6
Ratio	1.25	1.11	1.44	1.55	1.09

Between the twelfth and thirteenth photographic magnitudes the ratio had been found to be about 1.4, even when the Virgo and Fornax clusters of bright galaxies were removed from the statistics. For all galaxies together, between the fourteenth and the seventeenth magnitudes, it was also 1.4. The northern galactic hemisphere appears to be 40 percent richer than the southern throughout this volume of space; further out the difference disappears.

We should note that when we compare seventeenth-magnitude galaxies on one side of the Milky Way with the seventeenth-magnitude galaxies on the other, we are not dealing with short distances and localized irregularities. Such objects are in regions that are separated by nearly 500 million light-years. Whether the conspicuous population differences are to be accounted for by a great cloud of galaxies beyond the northern constellations, or are an indication of a major continuous south-to-north density increase, cannot now be determined. We first need to know the relative frequencies of the galaxies between the thirteenth and sixteenth magnitudes over large areas in the two hemispheres; and we shall also need to increase the number of regions examined for fainter galaxies before we can accept this south-north density gradient across the galactic plane as securely demonstrated.

Notwithstanding the lesser population of galaxies in the southern galactic hemisphere, which we find when intercomparing to the seventeenth magnitude the high-latitude regions of both hemispheres, the southern hemisphere has in the form of extensive clouds of galaxies at least two of the most conspicuous density irregularities. To one we have already referred in Chapter 5, where it was noted that even in relatively low galactic latitudes there is a rich background of faint and distant galaxies in the neighborhoods of the Andromeda Nebula and its associate, Messier 33. We cannot yet outline clearly the extent of this cloud of galaxies that extends away from the Milky Way through Andromeda into Triangulum, Pisces, and Pegasus. Tens of thousands of faint galaxies are involved. This string of galaxy clusters and clouds was first pointed out by W. E. Bernheimer and his associates at the Lund Observatory; it will doubtless be further unraveled in the Lick and Palomar galaxy surveys.

More clearly outlined than the metagalactic cloud just mentioned is the transverse stratum of galaxies that appears to be richest in the far-southern constellations of Pictor and Dorado, near the Large Magellanic Cloud. In this region, more than 200 million light-years away, it appears that the density of matter in space must be at least 50 percent higher than in other equally distant regions in the southern galactic hemisphere. Such differences are undoubtedly significant, since they are large-scale irregularities that must affect the large-scale operations of the Metagalaxy; but as yet we cannot interpret their message.

In the course of a few years all the southern sky will be more thoroughly mapped, and diagrams of the distribution of several millions of galaxies will be available. Then we shall see if there are definite and smooth transverse gradients in density from one part of the sky to another. And when enough careful work has been done on the magnitudes of the galaxies, it should also be clear whether or not important *radial* density gradients exist—that is, notable increases or decreases in the number of galaxies as one proceeds outward in any direction. Already the magnitude work on individual plates has shown that there are local radial irregularities—both smooth and freakish deviations from uniformity in the population density as we travel outward, counting the galaxies as we go.

Notwithstanding the widely distributed clusters and clouds of galaxies, a large-scale population uniformity does seem to exist. For if we consider still greater volumes of space, lumping together all the material for half a sky at a time, we find an average uniformity; that is, the density-gradient coefficient is 0.6. This result is based on a study of more than 100,000 galaxies measured by the Harvard observers, and it substantiates the earlier results by Hubble on his sample-area studies at Mount Wilson. The outcome is important enough to merit repeating: when very large areas and depths of the sky are considered, the mean value of the density-gradient coefficient is almost exactly 0.6, and therefore the space density of galaxies appears to be uniform *on the average* within a sphere of perhaps a billion light-years diameter, notwithstanding the presence of the large and numerous clusters of galaxies, the enormous clouds of galaxies, and extensive areas of low population as shown by the Lick Observatory charts (Fig. 79).

If there is a general thinning-out of galaxy population with distance, or a thickening-up, it is so small, and becomes effective only at such great and dim distances, that we cannot be sure of it. The brightnesses of galaxies are hard to measure accurately when they are fainter than the eighteenth magnitude, where our standards

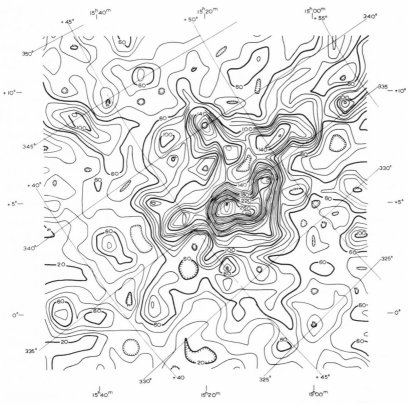

Fig. 79. A sample of the Lick Observatory maps of galaxy distribution. The great inequalities in the number of galaxies per square degree is illustrated; richest to poorest is about 10 to 1. The framing is shown in both galactic and equatorial coordinates. The center is at R.A. 5ʰ 20ᵐ, Dec. +5°.

of brightness are not nearly as safe as for brighter stars and galaxies. From surveys with the reflecting telescopes, Hubble found (after introducing corrections for red shift) what he believed may be a general radial gradient, which, over a distance of a quarter of a billion light-years, amounts to a density change of less than 20 percent. If fully established, such a radial gradient would be highly significant. Hubble naturally preferred to believe that the density is uniform. That would lead to simpler and more comfortable interpretations of the universe. Therefore, to eradicate the *apparent* increase in density with distance, and establish essential uniformity, he suggested the abandonment of the interpretation of the red shift as a velocity of recession, and the consequent abandonment of the hypothesis of the expanding universe; he would introduce in its place some new principle to account for the observed red shift.

But the evidence for Hubble's radial gradient was not very strong. The magnitude standards were not very secure. It can be readily shown that if the Mount Wilson surveys, on which the deduction was based, are analyzed separately for the northern and southern galactic hemispheres, the density-of-population increase on the north is negligible. Moreover, the total amount of the increase with distance, as originally deduced, is not impressive compared with other more localized gradients, some of which certainly cannot be erased by revision of the magnitude standards.

Radial density gradients, of course, are more difficult to establish than transverse gradients. My work on about 75,000 faint galaxies in the southern galactic hemisphere has shown a transverse gradient —a change in the frequency of galaxies per square degree in crossing a distance of some 500 million light-years—that is considerably greater than the general radial gradient originally suspected by Hubble, which led to his doubts concerning the existence of space curvature and of the alleged expansion of the universe. Later Hubble accepted the expansion as the proper interpretation of the red shift. Obviously we are not through with this business. The extensive galaxy surveys undertaken by Zwicky at Mount Palomar with the Schmidt telescopes (Fig. 80), and by Shane at the Lick Observatory with the Carnegie Astrograph (Fig. 81), will soon contribute importantly to our knowledge of population density and have a bearing on the nature of space-time.

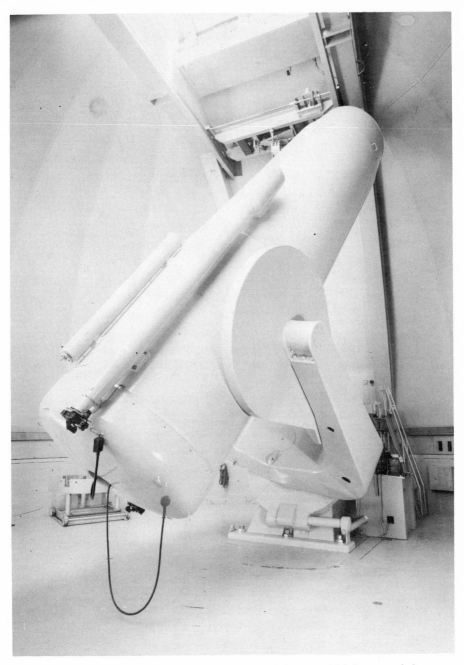

Fig. 80. The 48-inch Schmidt telescope on Mount Palomar, which has recorded
some millions of faint and distant galaxies.

Fig. 81.   The Carnegie Astrograph of the Lick Observatory.

The Motions of Galaxies

The foregoing discussion of density gradients in the Metagalaxy ends with references, not fully explained, to the expanding universe and the relativistic cosmogonies. It will be well to approach this subject by way of our knowledge of the motions of the galaxies.

Forty years ago, when we were not sure whether the spirals were near at hand, among the fainter stars in our own Galaxy, or were completely outside, it was natural that we should give them the cross-speed test for distance. The nearness of most near-by stars is easily discovered because their angular (cross) motions are large enough to be measured readily from year to year, or at least from decade to decade, or century to century. The more distant stars, just because they are distant, show little of this so-called proper motion or angular displacement, notwithstanding the fact that their cross speeds may be high. Proper motion, in fact, is a rough indicator of distance: small motion, far away; large motion, near by (or excessive natural speed).

A. van Maanen with the large reflectors at Mount Wilson made valuable tests of the cross motions of the nearer galaxies as a part of his elaborate program on the proper motions and distances of galactic stars. His measures on the nuclei of spiral nebulae showed no appreciable cross motions for the intervals of time separating his earliest and latest photographic plates. If the plates had been separated by 1000 or 10,000 years, the story would be different, because we are now pretty certain that the speeds of some of the galaxies are hundreds of miles per second, and in a long enough time measurable angular displacements must be possible.

If our present photographs of galaxies can be preserved for a few centuries, and duplicates then made for purposes of comparison, we should have valuable data on the cross currents in the Inner Metagalaxy, and we should have the means of analyzing the structure and dynamics of some of the nearer groups of galaxies. Moreover, we should be able, in a few thousand years, to learn as much about the cluster of bright galaxies in Virgo as we now know about the bright clusters of stars in Taurus—the Pleiades and the Hyades.

The apparent fixity on the sky of the faint external galaxies from year to year is so dependable, because of their great distances, that we can reverse the usual procedure and, instead of trying to measure their motions with reference to our standard neighboring stars, use the faint galaxies as fixed points of reference in space against which to measure the proper motions of our stellar standards. A far-sighted program of this kind has been undertaken in recent years at the Lick Observatory with the Carnegie Astrograph, which was constructed for the purpose of making use of the galaxies.

Although crosswise motions of the galaxies are now immeasurable, the motions in the line of sight, derived spectroscopically through the well-known Doppler principle, have been measured for several hundred of the brightest systems, thanks to the powerful spectroscopes on the largest telescopes. The work is not simple; and the accuracy is, of course, not nearly as high as for similar measures on neighboring stars.

The radial velocities (line-of-sight motions) now available are largely due to the work of one specialist, Milton Humason of the Mount Wilson and Palomar observatories. One of the most outstanding contributions yet made with the 100-inch and 200-inch

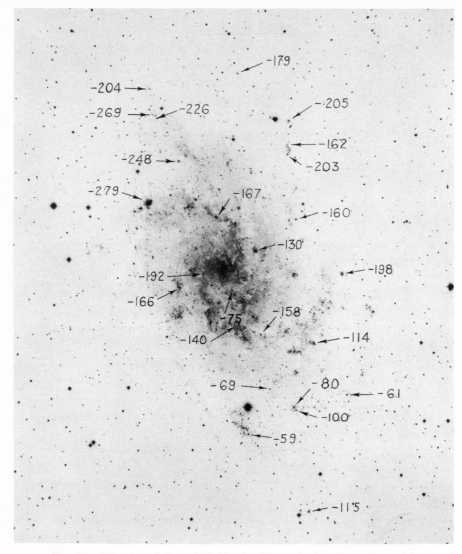

Fig. 82. Negative of the spiral Messier 33, marked to show the positions and velocities in kilometers per second of the nebulous patches that were measured by Mayall and Aller in their study of the rotation of the spiral. (Lick photograph, Crossley telescope.)

reflectors is Humason's measurement of the radial motions of very distant galaxies. Important pioneer work in this field was done by V. M. Slipher at the Lowell Observatory; and the Lick Observatory astronomers have also contributed significantly—for example,

Fig. 83. NGC 5128 is a large "problem" galaxy, studied by the Burbidges and others. Its distance is roughly 15 million light-years; velocity of recession, about 400 miles per second; rotation period, 55 million years. The mass is something like 200 billion suns, but whether it is one galaxy or two, perhaps a collision of a dark edge-on spiral with a great spheroidal, we do not yet know. (Harvard photograph, Rockefeller telescope.)

a study of the internal motions of Messier 33 (Fig. 82). Also note-worthy is the work at the McDonald Observatory on the queer galaxy NGC 5128 (Fig. 83) by the Burbidges and the spectrum work by G. Haro at Tonanzintla.

Large reflecting telescopes are essential to the work because the light that arrives from extragalactic space is feeble. In order that radial velocities may be determined from the spectrograms, the feeble light must be spread out sufficiently by the prism to show recognizable features in the spectra.

Red Shifts and Cosmogonies

The motion toward and from the observer is revealed in the faint spectra, according to the Doppler principle, by shifts of the spectral lines toward the blue and red ends of the spectrum, respectively. It was early discovered that except for a few nearby galaxies the spectrum shifts are all toward the red, and that the fainter the galaxy the more pronounced the red shift. Since faintness is associated with distance, it appeared, after sufficient observations had been accumulated, that the red shift was a fair indicator, if not an exact measure, of distance. Hubble derived the now well-known simple relation between the amount of red shift and the distance. Since we interpret that red shift for galaxies, as for the stars, as a direct result of motion away from the observer, the relation can be written as one between distance and speed in the line of sight.

Figure 84 diagrams an early version of the relation. It indicated that at a distance of 1 million light-years the galaxies recede at a speed of about 100 miles per second. At a distance of 2 million light-years, 200 miles per second; 10 million light-years, 1000 miles per second. But the revision of the zero point of the period-luminosity relation, described in Chapter 3, made revision necessary not only for distances of external galaxies, but also for the speed of expansion. The revising is not yet complete, since the scale of magnitude standards is not yet beyond correction. Tentatively we propose to accept a speed of expansion of 20 miles per second at a distance of 1 million light-years, and therefore a speed of 40 miles per second for a distance of 2 million light-years, and so on.

There was little tendency to question the interpretation of the red shift in terms of velocity so long as the measured speeds did not

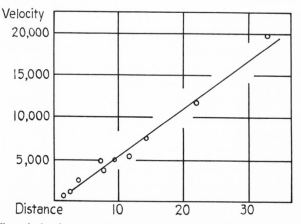

Fig. 84. The relation between the distances of galaxies, in megaparsecs, and the red shifts in their spectra, the latter expressed as velocity of recession in miles per second.

exceed a few hundred miles per second. Motions of that sort are known among the neighboring stars and are unquestioned. But when Humason's explorations reached objects more than 200 million light-years away, and the corresponding red shifts were indicating velocities of thousands of miles per second, some astronomers began to be uneasy; they wondered if out in those remote spaces something other than motion in the line of sight was producing the red shifts in the spectra. Velocities of 40,000 miles per second have now been attributed by Humason on the basis of his spectrographic work with the Hale 200-inch reflector to some of the faint galaxies, and W. A. Baum, with his photon-counter technique, has gone to higher speeds. Will those galaxies that we believe to be twice as far away as the remotest Humason measured move with speeds twice as great? And will those four to five times as far away show spectrum displacements to the red that would correspond to speeds of about 186,000 miles per second—the velocity of light?

The reason for the uneasiness is obvious. Scientists do not happily contemplate the possibility of real speeds greater than the velocity of light. But perhaps we are worried prematurely by this detail. The relation between distance and velocity, which has been shown to be approximately linear for the first 200 or 300 million light-years, is not yet accurately tested farther out. A deviation from the straight line seems inevitable; and already the 200-inch reflector on Palomar, equipped with the fastest possible spectrographic accessories, has shown that the red-shift relation, as we approach the billion-light-year distances, has become complicated. There is tentative evidence that the speed of expansion is now less than it was a billion years ago. Does this intimate that the Metagalaxy operates according to a pulsating model?

Not only do we need more of the extremely difficult measures of red shift for faint and distant galaxies, but we need, with equal urgency, accurate measures of magnitude for them. This second need emphasizes the importance of current research in photographic and other light-recording techniques.

Before further comment on the limiting velocity is ventured, it would probably be best to await the accumulation of additional observations bearing on the distribution, brightnesses, colors, and motions of the galaxies in distant regions of the metagalactic system. But the impatient scientists have proceeded to look for other interpretations of the red shift. For example, could not the light of distant galaxies grow red with age? Those quanta of radiation that ultimately make our spectrograms have spent a million centuries or so traveling in space since they were emitted from the stars in the distant galaxies. The intervening space has some dust and gas in it, and everywhere it is being crisscrossed by the emitted radiations of millions of stars. In consequence, could not earthward-bound quanta of radiation lose some of their energy and thereby increase in wavelength and move toward the red end of the spectrum?

Or what of the hypothesis that long ago the atoms of all the elements were larger or smaller than now? The radiation from distant parts of the Metagalaxy dates from a time in the remote past when the universe was younger. If in the interval of 100 million years or so the atoms have everywhere progressively changed in size or mass, there would likely be a corresponding change in the character of their radiations. We should not now without correction compare the shifted old light, which comes from atoms that were young when the radiation was emitted, with the new light from the old atoms of our terrestrial standards; the observed red shift may indicate not motion but the youth of the atoms whose antics produced the radiation. This, of course, is pure speculation, and not very intelligent.

There may be more sense to the speculative inquiry: Are we sure that the so-called fundamental "constants" of Nature (such as the velocity of light, the mass of the electron, its charge, the gravitational constant) are not in fact variable progressively over long intervals of time such as are concerned in the measurement of the light of eighteenth-magnitude galaxies? If one persists in the conviction that galaxies, stars, planets, animals, and even matter evolve, why exclude categorically the primitive physical constants from the process of change, from developing with time and space?

It goes without saying that, if the constants are not constant, we need no longer strain ourselves to interpret the red shift as due to a velocity of recession; or, for that matter, strive to interpret anything else on the cosmic scale.

Fortunately, there is one good reason for not now seeking furiously among these speculative alternatives in the hope of explaining away the red shift. Quite independently we have found in the theory of relativity an expectation that galaxies will scatter.

The theory does not certainly predict the speed of recession, but an expansion of the universe is quite consistent with the general theory, which has been thoroughly tested in the nearer parts of the astronomical world and generally accepted. However much we may worry about the implications of the relativity theory at the bounds of measurable space, we are still pretty well satisfied of its validity and of its necessity near at home. The motions of Mercury's orbit, the red shift of light emitted from the surfaces of high-density stars, and the "bending" of rays of starlight measured at the time of solar eclipses—these are all well-known astronomical demonstrations that Einstein's slight modifications of Newton's gravitational principles are justified.

Although the effects introduced by the theory of relativity are quite trifling in the solar system, and except for a few problems completely negligible in the Galaxy, they become of rather major importance in the outer Metagalaxy, and absolutely dominant when we try to figure out the total behavior of light, space, and time. Ambiguities arise at the boundaries partly because of the lack of decisive observations, and partly because the world now transcends our understanding—may always transcend it. We seek a satisfactory theoretical world model—something to visualize, if possible. To simplify the relevant and necessary mathematical and physical problems, certain assumptions and compromises must be made. We believe, for instance, that the truth about matter and motion in the universe lies between wholly motionless matter and wholly matterless motion; but how much of one, at this epoch, and how much of the other?

The necessary compromises create uncertainties and, supplemented by our present observational lacks, permit alternatives. We can logically deduce relativistic world models of various sorts. The universe on one model may alternately expand and contract. It may, according to another, have first contracted as the stars were forming from a vague primordium, and now, with a reversal of trend, have gone into indefinite expansion toward the zero of density, the nothingness of heat. Or it may have erupted into an indefinitely expanding world from an infinitely old condition of stale equilibrium; or originated catastrophically from a single all-inclusive primeval atom some billions of years ago.

Since sufficient space cannot be taken here to present the

relativistic cosmogonies and the many interesting contributions and arguments in recent years concerning the bearing of the relativity theory on various phases of cosmogony, the interested reader is referred to semipopular expositions by Eddington and Jeans, for example, Eddington's *Expanding Universe* (1933). And if his curiosity takes him deeper he should look at the more technical treatises by these same authors, and by de Sitter, Friedmann, Lemaître, Robertson, McVittie, Tolman, Milne, Einstein, Gamow, and Weyl, and the technical observational contributions by Hubble, Humason, Mayall, Shapley, and others. Bondi's *Cosmology* (Cambridge, 1952) is a good introduction that clearly presents both the primeval-atom theory of Lemaître and Gamow and the steady-state hypotheses of Bondi and Gold and of Hoyle.

Obviously the picture is not yet clear. The finiteness of the universe is not established; nor is the contrary. Eternity may be nonsymmetrical, differing in the forward aspect from the backward view. Time and labor will remove at least some of the ambiguities. The problems are not hopeless at all; but in a pessimistic mood Sir James Jeans wrote: "As you will see by now, there is an absolute feast of hypotheses to choose between. You may pin your faith to any one you please, but you must not be certain about any. Personally, I feel very disinclined to pin my faith to any; it seems to me that it is still very open to question whether space is finite or infinite, whether it is curved or flat, whether the so-called constants of Nature change in value or stand still—if indeed any of these questions have any meaning." And he ends by quoting Robert Louis Stevenson that "to travel hopefully is a better thing than to arrive."

Trends

In choosing the title for this section we are thinking about trends among the galaxies as well as in the thoughts and work devoted to them. It seems to be firmly established that galaxies are scattering in metagalactic space, and that the observable part of the universe is expanding. If we should choose to think of space as infinite, we could best say that the galaxies themselves are scattering in space, that we witness a material expansion. If we prefer to contemplate a finite spherical space-time, then it might be best to say that space itself is expanding, taking the galaxies along.

The growth of the universe in size is what we observe. We can reverse the chronology, with some interesting results. The universe we observe was smaller last year, and last century—ever smaller as we go back in time. Some billions of years ago (we cannot give an accurate figure) there must have been a pronounced cosmic congestion, for if the speeds throughout that long interval of time have for each individual galaxy been approximately as now, all were then close together. At that epoch in universal history the average density of matter in space was exceedingly high. Before the Expansion had far developed, the stars were probably in relatively frequent collision. That time would have been a favorable one for producing easily such fragments as planets, comets, meteors. Perhaps cosmic rays also originated from the violent explosion of the hypothetical primeval atom.

Even if the speeds throughout the past have not been constant at the present values, but have been, from the beginning of the Expansion, systematically accelerated, the Metagalaxy was certainly highly concentrated a few billion years ago. Apparently the only escape from admitting the existence of that condition is through denying that the red shifts indicate motions, or through questioning the present adequacy of our observations.

The age of the earth's oldest rocks and the abundance of radioactive elements remaining in earth and sun indicate the age of our planetary system, like the age of the Expansion, as a few billion years. Is this purely coincidental, or does it imply a causal connection of crowding with the origin of the earth? Also, the nature and behavior of star clusters in the Milky Way, as Bok has shown, point to a similar age for our Galaxy. It is a thought-provoking circumstance that earth, Galaxy, and the beginning of metagalactic expansion all appear to date from a rather recent epoch when sidereal material was highly concentrated. Are we finding the Age of the Universe?

Coincidences must not be taken too seriously, however, because it is hard to cramp the whole past life of the stars into a short span of a few billion years. It is difficult also to see how globular star clusters, and, as Zwicky has pointed out, the great spherical clusters of galaxies, could have such a recent origin. The trend of thought in recent years has been favorable to the "short" time scale suggested by the Expansion; but practically everyone is uncomfortable about its brevity. It does not seem sufficiently dignified that the majestic universe should measure its duration as scarcely greater

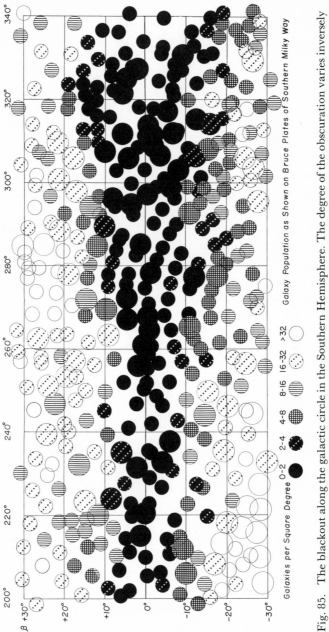

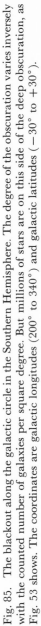

Fig. 85. The blackout along the galactic circle in the Southern Hemisphere. The degree of the obscuration varies inversely with the counted number of galaxies per square degree. But millions of stars are on this side of the deep obscuration, as Fig. 53 shows. The coordinates are galactic longitudes (200° to 340°) and galactic latitudes (−30° to +30°).

Fig. 86. Messier 22 in Sagittarius. Compared with spiral galaxies like Messier 31 (Andromeda Nebula), a part of which is shown in Fig. 87, the globular clusters have very little interstellar gas and dust. (Harvard photograph, Rockefeller telescope.)

than the age of the oldest rocks on this small planet's surface, or little greater than the age of the life in the crannies of the rocks.

New theories of the atomic nucleus and its evolution suggest the synthesis of the heavier chemical elements in the interiors of stars and in the explosions of novae and supernovae. All the kinds of atoms appear to have "descended" from hydrogen, the simplest. The relative abundance of the various atoms in stars, nebulae, and interstellar space is a rough measure of stellar ages. It suggests that the sun and planets originated out of cosmic gas and dust, such as that which blocks our view of the galactic center (Fig. 85), somewhat later than stars originated in dust-free globular clusters (Fig. 86) and in the nuclei of spiral galaxies. An age of 5 billion years is a round number for the sun's family; 10 or 12 billions for the oldest stars.

The measurements of radioactivity in terrestrial rocks, of the motions of galaxies, and of the speeds of dissolution of star clusters

Fig. 87. Supergiant stars involved in the dust and gas of the outer whorls of the Andromeda Nebula. (Mount Wilson photograph, 100-inch telescope.)

in our Milky Way, are all fairly clear-cut procedures. Those who measure such quantities feel that they qualify as scientists using scientific techniques. But when we begin to discuss the conditions that preceded the Expansion, or to inquire how primeval matter (for instance, neutral hydrogen) originated, whence came the matter from which eventually stars formed, and planets, and galaxies, we cannot claim full scientific endorsement.

The speculation of Canon Lemaître that a sort of radioactive explosion occurred in an all-including primeval atom, some 10 billion years ago, has attracted much attention because it involves the presumption of chaotic conditions that might help to solve some of the riddles of the origin of planetary systems. Eddington felt, however, that such an explosive origin was unnecessarily boisterous. He preferred the quiet of the static Einstein universe, with all major forces balanced. To quote him: "Accordingly the primordial state of things which I picture is an even distribution of protons and electrons, extremely diffuse and filling all (spherical) space, remaining nearly balanced for an exceedingly long time until its inherent instability prevails . . . There is no hurry for anything to begin to happen. But at last small irregular tendencies accumulate, and evolution gets under way. The first stage is the formation of condensations ultimately to become the galaxies; this, as we have seen, started off an expansion, which then automatically increased in speed until it is now manifested to us in the recession of the spiral nebulae [galaxies]. As the matter drew closer together in the condensations, the various evolutionary processes followed— evolution of stars, evolution of the more complex elements, evolution of planets and life."

We have been considering trends in the universe as a whole, and rather too soon passed from the fields of legitimate but laborious science to the attractive realm of cosmic speculation. Returning to the individual galaxies, we might inquire if there is evidence that they are changing in dimensions, or developing internally. Our interval of observation is of course too ridiculously brief for us to witness any progress; systematic changes can only be inferred.

For a few of the *Sc* spirals, supernova explosions have been recorded. In some of them two or three supernovae have appeared during our half-century of intermittent observing. If that frequency of violent upheaval has been maintained throughout the past 4 billion years, then a considerable proportion of all the stars may have experienced a change that is literally disastrous. Supernovation, as witnessed by us, may be a more emphatic factor in stellar and galactic evolution than we have heretofore supposed. This sort of convulsive evolution in the universe is worth closer watching; slow evolution is not necessarily predominant.

The galaxies rotate, and, according to the important work on the two bright spirals, Messier 31 and Messier 33 (Fig. 82), by Babcock, Wyse, Mayall, and Aller, the internal rotational motions are surprising, but not inconsistent with gravitational theory. Throughout much of our Galaxy, as in others, there must be potent shearing forces, sufficient to disrupt gradually the star clouds and many of the star clusters. Dissolution of internal stellar organizations appears inevitable. Bok has been able to predict the lifetimes of some star clusters in our own system. The trend in all these open spirals seems definitely to be in the direction of smoothing out the lumps. Are new lumps currently forming?

What will be the end product of the evolution of individual spirals, given enough time to carry through? Presumably there will be little serious disturbance from outside, because the galaxies are widely separated and are farther scattering. In multiples and clusters of galaxies, however, interpenetrations are likely, and have been proposed by Baade and Spitzer as the methods of clearing out the interstellar dust. Possibly the Magellanic Clouds occasionally make disturbing passages across our galactic plane; but in general a galaxy's internal evolution is its own private affair. Galaxies are not expanding; the mean density is too high.

The possibility that the end product of a spiral such as ours may be a spheroidal galaxy appears to be worth considering. It is proposed only as a working hypothesis. On such a plan, the evolutionary tendency among the galaxies would be from the Magellanic type (and such oddities as Fig. 88 shows for NGC 253) to the most open spiral (all of them characteristically full of supergiant stars, nebulosities, and bright star clusters), and thence through the other spiral forms, described in Chapter 1, to the elliptical and spherical systems—if not all the way, at least to type *Sa*. As mentioned above, spiral arms appear more as superficial structures in rich star fields than as ejections from a central nucleus (p. 141). Behind the spiral arms lies a fairly smooth spheroidal or discoidal galaxy.

In favor of the suggested evolutionary plan is the close resem-

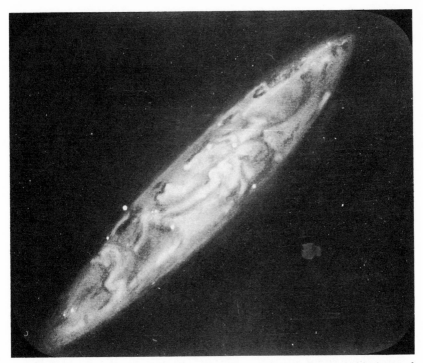

Fig. 88.   NGC 253, one of the large southern galaxies of remarkable internal structure and with no perceptible central nucleus. (Sketched from Harvard plates by Virginia McKibben.)

blance of the nuclei of spirals, in structure, size, and probably star content, to the main bodies of spheroidal galaxies and to the great globular star clusters like Omega Centauri. Another favoring circumstance is the progressive disappearance of the short-lived supergiant stars as the galaxies progress from irregular to spiral to spheroidal forms; there seem to be few supergiant stars in *Sa* spirals, and practically none at all in spheroidal galaxies.

The reverse direction of galaxy development suggested by Jeans, an evolution from compact spheroidal to open spiral, implies the appearance of supergiant stars and star clusters late in the history of a galaxy—a rather unlikely procedure. But however the galaxies have developed, and whichever the direction along the classification sequence, it is obvious that the time required for the transition from type to type must be so long that we hesitate to cramp the action within the span of a few billion years. Such a short time scale appears to be too confining for the evolution of ponderous galaxies.

Perhaps we should look at the development of large stellar systems as occurring in two stages, the first being the rapid and precipitate adjustment when the universe was young—an adjustment that quickly aggregated sidereal matter into unit galaxies of many sizes and forms, much as now prevails—and the other stage being that more deliberate dynamic and radiational process that is now going on and that in the long run, if the working hypothesis works, may tend to smooth out and perhaps round up the irregular galaxies and the much-nucleated open spirals, and move all nonspherical systems in the direction of the spheroidal galaxies.

It is puzzling to find many mixed double galaxies (see Fig. 13), with one an open spiral, the other a conservative spheroidal. They suggest a great difference in evolutionary stage, if not in age. Why the difference, if they have developed together? Clusters of galaxies pose the same problem. One thinks of the possibility of capture—a hypothetical process that is not dynamically very plausible. But the two-speeds plan, especially the production, by a primeval or secondary explosion, of full-blown spirals and spheroidals, is not very satisfactory either.

We may be driven, in our speculations, back to the long, long time scale, where there is duration enough to allow clusters and galaxies to evolve leisurely, while stars grow old and die, or blow up as supernovae and by way of reincarnation appear as second- or third-generation stars.

Meanwhile it will be refreshing to test some of these hypotheses with well-placed observations. Dozens of unsolved galactic problems can be outlined. We are far from finished, or from being finished, in this combat with the metagalactic mysteries. More measures, more correlations, more theoretical analyses—and then, if we like, a return to wistful speculation.

Index

Abell, G. O., 147
Absolute magnitude, 13; of average galaxy, 130, 147; of cepheid variables, 62f; of IC 1613, 118; of Sculptor and Fornax star clusters, 124
Absorption. *See* Space absorption
Achernar, 43
Age of universe, 156, 173; of planetary system, 173
Aller, L. H., 110, 166, 178
Almach, 105
Andromeda (constellation), 88, 107, 160
Andromeda Nebula, 2, 16, 28, 78f, 95, 100f, 103f, 123f, 147, 176, 178; absorption in region, 106; cepheid variables, 100, 106, 113; classification, 103, 105; densitometer tracing, 91, 108f; dimensions, 107f, 112; distance, 103f; faint companion, 79, 103; globular clusters, 100, 103f, 115; group of galaxies, 100; haze of stars, 91; internal motions, 178; luminosity, 112; map of region, 104f; mass, 109; mass/light ratio, 109f; measurement of size, 91; novae, 100, 113f; open clusters, 115; position, 103; star clouds, 114f; stellar population, 109, 113ff; supergiant stars, 114, 176; supernova, 100; tilt, 108; triple system, 100ff
Angular rotation of spirals, 6
Antares, 40
Anticenter, 91f
Apparent magnitudes, 13, 132
Aquarius, 158
Aquila, nova in, 114
Arcturus, 138f
Armagh Observatory, 115
Arp, H. C., 39, 83

Auriga, 91, 93
Average density of matter in space, 157

Baade, W., 42, 52, 81, 103, 105, 113, 117, 119, 123, 124, 143, 178
Babcock, Horace, 110, 178
Bailey, S. I., 33, 34, 51, 54, 120
Barnard, E. E., 55, 117
Barnard's galaxy (NGC 6822), 115ff
Barred spirals, 23f, 143
Baum, W. A., 83, 169
Bernheimer, W. E., 160
Betelgeuse, 40
Bok, B. J., 54, 173, 178
Bok, Mrs. P. F., 54
Bondi, H., 172
Bootes, 158
Boyden Observatory, 37, 68, 76
Bruce, Miss C., 30
Burbidge, E. M., 83, 167
Burbidge, G., 167

Canberra Observatory, 37
Candlepower, stellar, 5
Canes Venataci, 80, 158
Cannon, Miss A. J., 34, 37
Carpenter, E. F., 144
Cape Clouds, 28; *see also* Magellanic Clouds
Centaurus, 95f, 144
Cepheid variables, 6, 10f, 46, 89, 92, 104, 113; absolute magnitudes, 53f; in Andromeda Nebula, 100, 106, 113; distributions of periods, 46, 58ff; galactic system, 92f; frequency of periods, 60; in globular clusters, 86; in IC 1613, 118; in NGC 6822, 117; light curves, 63f; luminosity of cluster type, 89; in Magel-

181

Cepheid variables: lanic Clouds, 47f; number, 47; period-luminosity relation, 5, 48f, 57, 74; in Sculptor cluster, 122
Cetus, 158
Clark, A., 31
Clusters of galaxies, 148, 173; age, 173, 175; in Andromeda Nebula, 100, 103f, 115; diameters, 70f; in Fornax, 118, 123f; *see also* Fornax cluster of galaxies, Virgo cluster
of stars, 179f; in the Galaxy, 84; globular, 46, 73f, 80, 82f, 123, 173, 175; *h* and χ Persei, 78, 80; Hercules, 2, 36, 73f, 78; Hyades, 37, 78, 165; Kappa Crucis, 80f; in Magellanic Clouds, 36ff; Messier 3, 54f, 80; Messier 4, 81; Messier 22, 81, 175; in Messier 31, *see* Andromeda Nebula; Messier 62, 81; NGC 1910, 40f; NGC 2419, 76, 81; Omega Centauri, 75f, 80f, 179; open, 46, 83f, 115, 122f, 178; Pleiades, 2, 37, 78, 84, 165; in Sculptor cluster, *see* Sculptor cluster; 47 Tucanae, 29, 80f
Cluster-type variables, 11, 48, 52, 55, 80, 90
Coal Sack, 80
Color index defined, 8
Coma Berenices, 137f, 158
Comets, 173
Cordoba Observatory, 37
Corsali, A., 29
Cosmic rays, 173
Cosmic year, 87, 96
Crab Nebula, 3
Curtis, H. D., 6
Cygnus, 30, 95

Declination, 10
Delta Cephei, 10, 47, 53, 61
Density gradients, 148, 157ff
Density of matter, 148, 157
de Sitter, W., 172
de Vaucouleurs, G., 17, 23, 42, 145
Distances, stellar, 5, 8ff
Doppler principle, 8
Doppler shift, 167
Dorado, 29, 137, 160
Dreyer, J. L. E., 10, 115, 126, 127
Dwarf galaxies, 119, 139; Fornax cluster, 146f; frequency, 123; IC 1613, 42, 115f, 122, 124; in Leo, 123; NGC 147, 123; NGC 185, 123; NGC 6822, 115ff; Sculptor cluster, 118ff, 146
Dwarf stars, 15

Earth, age, 175; diagram of orbit, 8
Eclipsing binaries, 5, 48, 92
Eddington, A. S., 172, 177
Eighteenth-magnitude survey, 148ff, 158f
Einstein, A., 171, 177

Ellipsoidal galaxies. *See* Spheroidal galaxies
Eta Carinae, 14
Evans, D. S., 124
Expanding universe, 151ff
Extragalactic nebula, 17

Feast, M. W., 39
Flammarion, C., 30
Fornax cluster of galaxies, 137, 145ff, 159
Fornax star cluster, 118, 123f
Friedmann, A., 172

Galactic circle, 128f
Galactic latitude, 10, 84
Galactic longitude, 10
Galactic system. *See* Galaxy
Galaxies, absolute magnitude of average, 130; angular diameters, 7f, 15, 127; angular rotation, 6; bright, distribution, 126ff, 158f; magnitudes, 127f, 130ff; classification, 17ff; clusters, *see* Clusters of galaxies; colors, 140f; density gradients, 148; distribution, 93, 127ff, 148ff, 158ff; double, 111, 180; dwarf, *see* Dwarf galaxies; faint, distribution, 148ff, 158ff; Magellanic-type, 17, 95, 116, 122, 139, 178; magnitudes as distance criteria, 7; masses, 157; metagalactic cloud, 107, 144f, 160; nomenclature, 10, 17; rotation, 178; radial motions, 165; red shift, 6ff, 162, 167ff, 173; spectra, 140, 167ff; spheroidal, *see* Spheroidal galaxies; spiral, *see* Spiral galaxies; supergiant stars, *see* Supergiant stars; surveys, 18, 127ff, 135, 148ff, 158ff; types, 16ff
Galaxy (Milky Way system), 73ff, 124; age, 173; boundaries, 90ff; classification, 95; definition of neighborhood, 99f; diameter, 90; distance of center, 96; nucleus (center), 84f, 93, 95f; obscuration in, 91; rotation, 44, 86f; shape, 86; size, 6; star clouds, 86
Gamow, G., 172
Gaposchkin, S. I., 40
Gemini, 91
"General Catalogue" of J. Herschel, 126, 135
General luminosity curve, 66, 70
Globular clusters, 46, 73f, 80, 82f, 123, 173, 175
Gold, T., 172
Greenstein, J. L., 55
Grus, 137
Guthnick, P., 55

H II regions, 115
Haro, G., 140, 167
Harvard Observatory, 30, 74, 91f, 118, 123, 139, 160, 179; ADH telescope, 14, 29,

Harvard Observatory:
  31, 33, 47, 77, 93; Agassiz Station, 92, 94, 141, 148ff; Arequipa Station, 31; AX camera, 43; Bache (8-inch) telescope, 59; Bruce (24-inch) telescope, 22, 31ff, 47, 93, 120, 122, 143, 148ff, 152f, 155f; galactic surveys, 18, 127ff, 148ff, 158ff; Jewett-Schmidt telescope, 93; Metcalf (12-inch) telescope, 142; Metcalf (16-inch) telescope, 75, 93f, 148, 150; Oak Ridge Station (now Agassiz), 89, 104, 124, 142; Rockefeller (60-inch) telescope, 5, 11, 21, 37, 41, 75, 121; South African (Boyden) Station, 89, 92, 124; variable-star surveys, 90
Heidelberg, 115
Henry Draper Catalogue, 37
Hercules cluster, 2, 36, 73f, 78
Herschel, J., 30, 32, 74, 82, 126, 127
Herschel, W., 3, 74, 82, 126, 127
Herschel telescope, 82
Hertzsprung, E., 50, 63
Hodge, P., 123
Hogg, Mrs. H. S., 75
Holmberg, E., 111, 138, 141, 144
Hoyle, F., 172
Hubble, E. P., 3, 6, 17, 18, 23, 113, 115ff, 124, 135, 137, 141f, 150, 160, 162, 168, 172
Humason, M. L., 140, 165, 166, 169, 172
Hyades cluster, 37, 78, 165
Hydrogen, 173, 177
Hydrogen haze, 46

IC 10, 124
IC 342, 124
IC 1613, 42, 115f, 122, 124
IC 5152, 124
Index Catalogue (IC), 10, 126f
Inner Metagalaxy, 126ff
Irregular galaxies, 17, 95, 116, 122, 139, 178
Irwin, J. B., 39
Island-universe hypothesis, 2, 3, 6

Jeans, J. H., 172, 179
Jodrell Bank, 108

Kant, I., 2, 6
Kappa Crucis, 80f
Kapteyn, J. C., 12
Katz, L., 137
Kepler's Nova, 114
Kerr, F. J., 42
Kiloparsec, 10
Kraft, R. P., 39

Lampland, C. O., 81
Large Magellanic Cloud, 43, 58f, 160f; bar (axis), 34f, 56; diameter, 30; distance, 36, 41f; general luminosity curve, 67, 69f; giant and supergiant stars, 66f, 69; globular clusters, 36ff, 46; light curves of cepheids, 64; luminosity curve, 67, 69; number of known variables, 56; open clusters, 37, 39f, 70ff; period distribution of variables, 61; period-luminosity relation, 46ff; position, 35; radial velocity, 44; S Doradus, 40f; tilt, 42; *see also* Magellanic Clouds
Larink, J., 55
Leavitt, Miss H. S., 32ff, 48, 49, 51, 56
Lemaître, G., 172, 177
Lick Observatory (Mount Hamilton), 30, 44, 103, 110, 117, 123f, 126, 160ff, 166; Carnegie astrograph (20-inch), 150, 162, 164f; Crossley reflector, 166
Light curve, 11
Light-year, 10
Lindblad, B., 141, 142
Lindsay, E. M., 37
Local group of galaxies, 100, 115, 123, 145, 147
Long-period variables, 11, 48, 89
Loop Nebula (30 Doradus), 36f
Lowell Observatory, 166
Luminosity curve, 66
Lund Observatory, 97, 160
Lundmark, K., 3, 6, 17
Luyten, W. J., 44
Lynx, 76, 137

Magellan, 29
Magellanic Clouds, 2, 25, 27ff, 45ff, 80, 100, 115, 117, 122ff, 136, 160, 178; dimming by space absorption, 39; distances, 36, 41; from galactic plane, 44; eclipsing stars, 48; general luminosity relation, 66ff; motions, 44; positions, 35; radial velocities, 44; star clusters, 36ff, 46, 70ff; stellar spectra, 37; variable stars, 33f, 39, 46ff; *see also* Large *and* Small Magellanic Cloud
Magellanic-type galaxies, 17, 95, 116, 122, 139, 178
Magnitude, 7; absolute, 13; apparent, 13
Martyr, P., 28
Mayall, N. U., 17, 23, 110, 142, 166, 172, 178
McDonald Observatory, 167; 82-inch telescope, 101
McVittie, G. C., 172
Median apparent magnitude, 53
Megaparsec, 10, 130f
Mercury's orbit, 171
Messier, C., 10, 74, 82
Messier 3, 54f, 80
Messier 4, 81
Messier 11, 80
Messier 13 (Hercules cluster), 2, 36, 73f, 78
Messier 22, 81, 175

Messier 31. *See* Andromeda Nebula

Messier 32, 27, 101, 103, 112f, 115, 124

Messier 33, 28, 100, 103f, 112f, 124, 144, 160, 166f, 178

Messier 42 (Orion Nebula), 3f, 36, 78, 80

Messier 55, 11

Messier 57, 3f

Messier 59, 19

Messier 60, 25, 28

Messier 62, 81

Messier 81, 102

Messier 83, 21, 22

Messier 101, 100ff, 141

Messier's Catalogue 74

Metagalaxy, 12, 100, 116, 125ff, 153f, 157, 160, 164, 171, 173; census, 126ff, 148ff; expansion, 154, 164f, 173; structure, 157ff

Meteors, 173

Michell, J., 6

Microdensitometer, 141f

Miczaika, G. R., 7, 55

Milne, E. A., 172

Mirach, 104f

Morgan, W. W., 17, 23, 140

Mount Hamilton. *See* Lick Observatory

Mount Wilson and Palomar Observatories, 83, 103, 117f, 122ff, 126, 136f, 139f, 140, 158, 160, 162f, 165; Hale (200-inch) telescope, 4, 20, 24, 55, 76, 92, 102, 131, 144, 169; Hooker (100-inch) telescope, 19, 25, 103, 113, 117, 119, 150, 176; 60-inch telescope, 88, 96, 116; Schmidt (48-inch) telescope, 147, 150, 163

Mulders, G. F. W., 137

Müller, Th., 55

Nail, V. McK., 40, 58, 179

Nebula, anagalactic, 3; Andromeda, *see* Andromeda Nebula; Crab, 3; Eta Carinae, 14; extragalactic, 3, 114f; Loop, 36f; Orion, 3f, 36, 78, 80; Ring, 3f

New General Catalogue (NGC), 10, 126f

Newton, I., 15, 171

NGC objects in Fornax cluster, 146

NGC 185, 147

NGC 205, 103, 112f, 115, 124

NGC 221 (M 32), 27, 101, 103, 112f, 115, 124

NGC 224. *See* Andromeda Nebula

NGC 253, 178f

NGC 891, 88

NGC 1042, 171

NGC 1316, 146

NGC 1866, 40

NGC 1910 (S Doradus), 40f

NGC 2419, 76, 81

NGC 2427, 124

NGC 3115, 19

NGC 3379, 19

NGC 4027, 143

NGC 4038–9, 143

NGC 4565, 20

NGC 4594, 92

NGC 4621 (M 59), 19

NGC 4647, 25, 27

NGC 5128, 143, 167

NGC 6720, 3f

NGC 6822 (Barnard's galaxy), 115ff

NGC 6946, 124

NGC 7582, 145

NGC 7590, 145

NGC 7599, 145

NGC 7793, 22

Nichol, J. P., 3

Novae, 11, 53, 89, 175; in Andromeda Nebula, 100, 113f; in Aquila, 114; in Messier 33, 114f

Obscuration by dust and gas, 86, 135ff, 142, 144, 174ff, 178

Omega Centauri, 78f, 80f, 179

Oort, J. H., 141

Open cluster, 46, 83f, 115, 122f, 178

Ophiuchus, 84

Öpik, E., 110

Orion Nebula, 3f, 36, 78, 80

Page, T., 111, 144

Parallax, stellar, 8

Paraskevopoulos, J. S., 37

Parsec, 9, 54

Patterson, Miss F. S., 141

Pegasus, 96, 158, 160

Period of variable star, 11

Period-luminosity relation, 5, 39, 46, 48f, 66; for Barnard's galaxy, 118; in Magellanic Clouds, 46, 48ff

Peripheral band of obscuration, 88, 91

Perseus, *h* and χ, 80, 95

Pickering, E. C., 31, 48

Pictor, 160

Pigafetta, A., 29

Pisces, 158, 160

Photometer, 10, 91

Planets, 173, 177

Plate spirals, 143

Pleiades, 2, 37, 78, 84, 165

Polaris, 47, 53, 61

Pretoria Observatory. *See* Radcliffe Observatory

Primeval atom, 177

Proctor, R. A., 3, 135, 136

Proper motion, 8, 165f

Radcliffe Observatory (Pretoria), 37, 44, 48, 119, 124

Radial velocity, 8; galaxies, 165f; Virgo cluster, 140
Radio, 91, 95, 108f
Radioactivity, 173, 175, 177
Randers, G., 141
Reaves, G., 123
Red shift, 6ff, 162, 167ff, 173
Region of avoidance, 135ff
Regulus, 138f
Relativity theory, 171
Reynolds, J. H., 17
Right ascension, 10
Ring Nebula, 3f
Ring-tail galaxy (NGC 4038–9), 143
Robertson, H. P., 172
RR Lyrae stars, 11

Sagittarius, 30, 74, 81, 84, 86, 91, 94, 96, 117
Sample-areas survey, 135, 159
Sandage, A. R., 39, 83
Sawyer, H. A., 104
Sawyer, Miss H. B. (Mrs. H. S. Hogg), 55
Schlesinger, F., 12
Schmidt camera, 81, 83, 147
Schwarzschild, M., 55
Scorpion, 81
Scorpius, 84, 94
Sculptor cluster, 16, 118f, 146; cepheids, 122; distance, 122, 124
Sculptor (constellation), 158
Scutum, 30, 94, 96
S Doradus, 40f
Seyfert, C. K., 140
Shane, C. D., 126, 162
Shapley-Ames catalogue of bright external galaxies, 17, 127ff, 132, 137
Shapley, H., 37, 40, 51, 52, 55, 58, 108, 135, 158, 162, 172
Sirrah, 104f
Sinton, W. M., 7
Slavenas, P., 55
Slipher, V. M., 142, 166
Small Magellanic Cloud, 43, 116; cepheid variables, 58f; diameter, 30; distance, 41f; obscuration, 65, 106f; period distribution of variables, 57ff; period-luminosity relation, 46ff, 74; position, 29; radial velocity, 44; tilt, 42; wing, 42f; see also Magellanic Clouds
Smith, S., 140
Space absorption, 39, 103, 106f, 117, 124, 129, 132, 141, 148
Space-density parameter, 132f, 152ff
Space-time, 156
Space reddening, 141, 170
Spectral classes, 3, 8; galaxies, 3, 140; P Cygni, 40; stars, 8, 140
Spectroscope, 3, 7
Spheroidal galaxies, 18, 139, 178ff; classification, 18f; luminosity curve, 70; relative frequency, 17, 116, 123
Spica, 138
Spiral galaxies, 6, 17, 19, 20ff, 80, 139, 144, 179f; angular rotation, 6; arms, 23, 142, 178; classification, 21f; motions, 178; "plate" spirals, 143; relative frequency, 17, 116, 141; supernovae, 177
Spitzer, L., 178
Star haze, 46, 89f, 93, 109; around Andromeda Nebula, 90f, 108f; exploration, 93; around Magellanic Clouds, 46; around Messier 33, 113; thickness, 90
Stebbins, J., 140
Stellar distance, 5, 8
Stephan's quintet, 95f
Stevenson, R. L., 172
Sun, eclipses and relativity test, 171; relative luminosity, 16; supergalazy, 145
Supergiant stars, 142, 178f; absence from spheroidal galaxies and globular clusters, 70, 178f; in Andromeda Nebula, 176; census in Large Magellanic Cloud, 67; luminosity curve, 66f, 69
Supernovae, 40, 175, 177f; in Andromeda Nebula, 100
Surveys of galaxies, 18, 127ff, 135, 148ff, 158ff
Swedenborg, E., 6
Sweeney, Miss J., 135
Swope, Miss H. H., 104

Taurus, 91, 93, 165
Thackeray, A. D., 119
Thirteenth-magnitude survey, 127ff
30 Doradus (Loop Nebula), 36f
Tolman, R. C., 172
Tonanzintla, 140, 167
Toucan, 29
Triangulum, 100, 107, 160
Trumpler, R. J., 39

Ursa Major, 137, 158

van de Kamp, P., 15
van den Bergh, S., 39, 83
van Maanen, A., 165
Van Vleck Observatory, 9
Variable stars, cepheids, see Cepheid variables; cluster-type, 11, 48, 52, 55, 80, 90; in clusters of stars, 6, 10f, 40, 50, 54f, 80; distance, maximum, 90; distribution as function of latitude, 93ff; eclipsing, 5, 11; irregular, 92; light curves, 11, 47, 63ff, 106; long-period, 11, 48, 92; in Magellanic Clouds, 33f, 39, 46ff, 57ff; in Messier 3, 54f; period, 11; period-luminosity relation, see Period-luminosity relation; RR Lyrae, 11; S Doradus, 40f; velocity curve, 11

Virgo cluster of galaxies, 113, 123, 136ff, 147, 158, 165; classification of galaxies, 139f; colors, 140f; diameters of galaxies, 142; position, 137ff; spectra, 140f; speeds and masses, 140; spread in luminosity, 147
Virgo (constellation), 137, 158
von Humbolt, A., 3
von Zeipel, H., 55

Weyl, H., 172
Whipple, F. L., 140
Whitford, A.E., 140

Wilson, A. G., 123
Wilson, R. E., 44, 52
Wolf, M., 115
Wyse, A. B., 110, 178

Yale Observatory, 12

Zero-point, magnitude system of Shapley-Ames catalogue, 128; period-luminosity curve, 52f, 105; space-density relation, 155
Zwicky, F., 126, 144, 145, 162, 173